Journey to Awakening

Journey to Awakening

Mary Nelson

Overlook Publishing
Steamboat Springs, CO

Journey to Awakening
by Mary Nelson
Copyright © 2022 by Mary Nelson

All rights reserved. No part of this book may be reproduced in any written, electronic, recording, or photocopy form without the prior permission of the publisher except for the inclusion of brief quotations in a review.

ISBN: 978-0-9848419-1-2 (print)
Library of Congress Control Number: 2020924221

Overlook Publishing
Steamboat Springs, CO

Editing by Melanie Mulhall, Dragonheart
www.DragonheartWritingandEditing.com
Developmental Editing by Joya Stevenson
www.book-editing.com/joya-stevenson
Book Design by Bob Schram, Bookends Design
www.BookendsDesign.com

Joel Goldsmith quote used with permission.
Gary Crowley quote used with permission.

Printed in the United States of America
First Edition

Dedication
To all the expressions of God
who seek to awaken

Contents

Preface 1
Introduction 11
1. Another View of Life 15
2. What Is Spirit and Who Am I? 25
3. Getting on the Moving Sidewalk 33
4. Doing Versus Being 43
5. Connecting Body, Mind, and Spirit 53
6. The Body 57
7. The Mind 63
8. Mind-Based Beliefs 69
9. Releasing the Unintended 77
10. Living from the Inside Out 87
11. Spiritual Paths 97
12. Stopping the Mind 109
13. Developing Your Intuition 119
14. My Awakening 135
Acknowledgments 143
About the Author 145

Preface

How's your life? Going smoothly? Somewhat stressed? Really painful? We've all heard it and said it: Life is hard. It's not meant to be that way. The world wasn't created to run on chaos. But if we look back over hundreds and thousands of years, it's been pretty rocky.

Can you change that? Not for others, but a resounding yes for yourself. You can change your life. Whether you struggle with relationships, finances, health, or loneliness, you can transform all of that into peace. All you have to do is wake up. That means open your heart and mind to find out who you truly are—because you are more than you can even imagine.

What does it mean to have a spiritual awakening? It happens differently for each person, but the basic unifying event is the sudden loss of a sense of self and an opening to our uniqueness as an indispensable part of the entire universe. A spiritual awakening is the experiential realization that you are not the "you" that you think you are. Instead, you are—and you always have been—an expression of the Creator of all life, who lives through you and as you. Although an awakening will usually be spontaneous, living it comes as a process. It is what I call a *spiritual journey*.

For me, the journey actually began on a sunny afternoon when I was five years old and seeking the unconditional love of nature as an escape from the loneliness and fear I felt within our house. I was lying in my backyard, gazing at a deep blue sky filled with mounds of white billowy clouds. The green of the grass and the crispness of the leaves offered both order and a cushion to the wounded and hard edges of my heart. As I felt the inviting warmth of the sun on my body and the grass beneath my legs, I said to the sky, "I wish somebody loved me."

In a clear and authoritative voice only audible internally, the sky answered, "I love you, little girl."

I knew it was God, but I didn't know his name. It would be another twenty-five years before I made that intense connection again, but when I did, I began a journey that transformed everything about me.

Everyone is on a path because life is a journey of growth on all levels (physical, mental, emotional, and spiritual). To function and grow in our human lives, we learn the basics: We develop our personalities and our perceptions of the world; we learn to manage within cultural systems; and we hone our ability to interact with other people. On our journeys, we develop a sense of who we are in our body, mind, and experiences. We also struggle through painful situations because from birth to death, we evolve.

We may or may not be aware of the journey. We may or may not enjoy it or like the results. Because we are diverse and individual, some of us desire to be aware of growth and change. Others have no interest in examining themselves. They would rather just live and be happy. But the truth is that none of us gets to be totally happy. We all have to struggle. How can we know what *happy* is if we don't know *sad*? How can we know anything if we don't know its opposite? Up, down. Left, right. In, out. Dark, light. Life is actually a complete lesson in opposites.

So it is with awakening. In a moment, or by a process, we find out that who we really are is the opposite of who we think we are. And what if real life is the opposite of all that previously seemed so true? What if our "real life" is not about our human identities but our spiritual ones? What if there were a fuller, richer way to live? What if we could have more answers and be more at peace? What if we didn't have to figure it all out?

All of these what-ifs are what happens when we wake up because we then live from the fullness of God instead of living from our human limitations. We live not just *from* but *as* God in divine fullness. When I am asked how I learned what I did and how I let go of what I believed, my answer is, "I learned who God is and who I am not."

Most of us have had some experience beyond the realm of the senses. It may have occurred as a sensation or a synchronicity. We get goose bumps when someone says something or we happen to think of someone at the exact moment they call. The point is that few of us actively pursue that "other thing" that created the chill or gave us foreknowledge. We understand that the experience isn't coming from us, although it is coming to and through us, but we just think, *Oh, that was weird*, and we do not give it another thought. How many of us pursue the origins of the thought, knowledge, or experience and trace it to the source from which it came?

The key is that our journeys can shift from the ordinary and the struggle to becoming amazing, freeing, and spontaneous. We just need to begin to pay attention so we can wake up. We are living in the illusion that we are separate from God, the Creator. We are not. Our unique being is the visible and tangible form of God. He created all that is. All that exists is infused with and by his life, and that includes us.

For thirty years, I lived in my body, used my mind, and pretty much ignored my spirit. And even though I always had a sense of there being something more to life than what we perceive, I never actively searched for it. My life unfolded as it was meant to—all leading to the moment when I would open my heart.

On March 29, 1979, I had a profound encounter with God. It happened when all the security on which I depended disappeared. Within one week, everything had crashed around me, and it was more than I could handle. I was divorced and raising three young children. Their father was not paying child support. Suddenly I had to give up my job because the company for which I worked was going to move out of state, and I didn't want to uproot my children. Early that same week, I ended an unhealthy relationship. Desperately seeking comfort and needing help, I called each member of my family. One by one, my pleas for their support and comfort fell on deaf ears. No one was willing to come. There was no money, no help, no comfort, and nowhere to turn. I didn't have any answers, and I felt as helpless as a bereft child, which internally was the truth. I just didn't know it then.

I fell apart.

In a desperate attempt to gain control, I asked myself how these events had created such overwhelming anguish and fear. I didn't think it was normal, and I didn't think other adults would react as I had. Clearly, I was incapable of handling such an overload of problems. I was facing them as an emotionally damaged child instead of as an adult. I had buried memories of childhood abuse and didn't know that I was navigating with defective radar. The pain was too strong, the issues were too big, and the lack of support only confirmed what the abuse had drilled into me: I was not worth it.

In that moment of total despair, I also couldn't see that my difficulty and turmoil were designed to make me pursue what life is all about. But before I could move in a new direction, I had to come to the end of myself. My new life would begin with a deep desire to die.

I went into my bedroom, locked the door, sat on the floor with my legs crossed, and began to breath slowly. Consumed by fear and pain, I was trying to find any kind of hope or peace by just being quiet.

I began to picture slitting my wrist and became enthralled with the vision of a shiny silver blade and bright red blood. It was pulling at me, enticing me to embrace an answer that would end my pain. In that moment, I wanted to die. Yet the more mesmerized I became by the thought and picture of ending my life, the more I felt myself sink into a deep black hole. It was as if I were being sucked into a never-ending void.

With a sudden, overwhelming sense of fear at being powerless to resist the pull into emptiness, I cried out, "God, if you are really there, if you are really real, I will be anything you want me to be if you will just take this pain away."

Instantly, I was plucked from the darkness and surrounded by blinding white light. My body and emotions were bathed in peace while I sat in awe of a presence that had suddenly filled everything, everywhere. I was consumed by an awareness of an "other" essence surrounding me. It overpowered me and had no limits. It was all, and I was only watching it.

Bathed in the light and peace of this presence, I experienced none of the pain, fear, or turbulent drama that had consumed me seconds before. I was just there, but it wasn't the same me who was sitting on the floor. For the first time, I began to lose a sense of myself. Instead, the all-consuming presence of God settled upon me.

Eventually, I again became aware of myself, in my body, sitting on the floor. But white light was still flooding the room and I spoke to it. "Holy cow. You are really real." I was fully experiencing Life beyond human expression, and it was filling me and everything in my room. I was in it and awed by the pure form of peace that I couldn't explain. My surrender had come from the depth of my pain, my prayer, and the fact that I had been absorbed by the Light—if only for a few seconds.

In *The Power of Myth* Joseph Campbell says that myths show us that when things are darkest, transformation—light—will come forth. But this was no myth. I was experiencing this in a very real and literal way. The light had consumed everything: the darkness, my pain, and me.

Though I did not know it at the time, when I promised to be anything God wanted me to be, I had unconditionally relinquished every ounce of my being. So deep was my cry that in that instant, my life no longer belonged to me. Without understanding all that it meant, I had handed over control and ownership of everything. My new life would take me from the perception of being Mary, a mere human being, to the truth of my real self as an expression of the only Life that exists. In the course of my journey, I lost my personal sense of self.

It has been forty-one years since that life-changing experience. Yet, that one moment in 1979 unfolded into a journey beyond anything I could have imagined. When I was growing up, I wanted to be a doctor. Once I married, I wanted to be a stay-at-home mom. I wanted the life of June Cleaver. Nowhere in my wildest dreams could I have imagined the new course my life would take. It would be directed by an intense spiritual journey filled with experiences that were a million times bigger than goose bumps. And in no way did I ever think I'd want to share them as I am doing here.

Yet that one encounter with God was the beginning of a process that completely transformed me and the whole of my life. It took many years, but in the end, I completely lost a sense of self and became who I was meant to be. Not only did I begin to live from the core of my being and depend only on Spirit for guidance, I let go of my mind's idea of who I was and what I needed to do.

I woke up. The idea of an ego-self (the part of us we consider our identity) with a personal mind disappeared. I lost the feeling of being Mary and my personal sense of identity. Instead, I began to know and feel myself as a creation of the only Life (God) that exists. I realized that

I am an expression of God, born of the Conscious Energy that created the world.

This awakening didn't happen all at once. I alternately dove into the transformation and fought it. There were times when I would very adamantly say, "Sorry God, I need a break." But I was always pulled back to my spiritual journey because when you find home, you want it. I had made the connection and I couldn't live without it.

It took me thirty years to let go, to die to the self and let God live as me. It happened with a hint here, a picture there, and experiences that constantly said, *See, Mary. I am in control. I am your life. Trust that. You don't have to live in struggle or pain.*

It doesn't have to take as long for you as it did for me. My purpose in writing this book is to help you embrace your spiritual journey and open your heart to transformation. In this book, I share the things I have learned and what I have done to stay on the path. I talk about my awakening as well as my own resistance and what I did to dissolve it. I share how I moved out of the situations and relationships in my life that caused pain or discomfort. There are also tips and techniques that can help you see yourself as already whole and complete. In this way, you may discover a deeper experience of life and of yourself. It is an experiential journey, and it is unique for everyone. Yours is awaiting you.

Throughout the book I refer to "God" because it is the most commonly used term for the divine. I am not speaking of an entity that sits on a throne. "God" is essentially everything. Different people call this power that is called God by other terms, including Universe, Divine

Consciousness, Source, Energy, Presence, and Essence. Please feel free to translate my most commonly used terms—God, Divine Consciousness, and Spirit—however it is comfortable for you. It does not matter. It's all God. Besides, God never said, "Hmm. When I get around to creating people, I think I'll tell them to call me God."

My background is in Christianity, and occasionally I refer to scripture. But it is my belief that the journey to wisdom and awakening begins at the bottom of a mountain that may be ascended from multiple places, sides, and paths. Each view of the mountaintop is different, just as each climb takes place from its own direction. But in the end, the top is the top.

My journey has included many illogical, otherworldly, and mystical experiences. They happened partly because I was chosen to have this particular journey and partly because I was open to it. Your experiences will be as specific to you as mine have been to me. My journey is not yours. The circumstances and ways in which people experience spiritual awakening are different for each of us. I cannot guarantee that mystical events will happen for you, although if you want them to happen, I hope they will. Each person's path home is unique, just as each of us is unique. I encourage you to open to your special journey and to embrace whatever unfolds, however it does, and to wake up according to the plan for you.

By sharing my experiences, the wisdom I have gained, and some of my practices, my hope is to help others embrace the journey, wake up, and live in peace feeling a deep sense of your true essence—the very mind, body, and spirit of God.

Introduction

WHO AM I . . . REALLY? Are my dreams just flowers that bloom in my mind reaching for the sun, craving to be watered but doomed to die? Is there more to me than the work I do, raising the children I have, and being a great spouse and friend? What about the book I'm writing, picture I'm painting, and garden I work so hard to make beautiful? What about all the mistakes I've made? The wrong lover. The wrong job. The wrong friends. What about the less life-altering mistakes, like the wrong vacation spot or purchasing the wrong dress or suit? Are these the things that define me? My mistakes? Am I just a creation of the choices I make?

Who am I, anyway? Do I need to know?

Those are the kinds of questions many of us ask ourselves, and they're heavy questions. Let's lighten up. It's not as serious as we think. We are all doing exactly what we are meant to be doing in this moment; however, we can do better by seeing more.

In 2005, I was in Sedona, Arizona, and had the opportunity to attend a workshop given by Dannion Brinkley, author of *Saved by the Light*. Dannion was pronounced clinically dead on two different occasions. Once he was electrocuted while working on a home project. The other time he died on the operating table. He died, went to the "other side," and came back—twice—bearing clues for all of us to see greater purpose in our lives. He shared that we chose to come here and were chosen to come here. He told us to find out why and get on with it.

We are not here randomly. We have been created, and we have chosen to come to Earth. We aren't just who we see in the mirror. We're not just a body with a mind and emotions, a mortal being that perishes. And we certainly aren't just the problems we have. We are purposeful creations in a beautiful scenario called life. We are visible expressions of the Spirit of God, which is immortal and imperishable. We are the balloon, and God is the air that gives it form. We are so much more than we can imagine, and we can find that truth of ourselves by going past our concepts and looking deeper.

We get so caught up in our human sensations and stories that we think we are defined by them. We have lost the truth of who we are because we have been trained to believe it is our world and our story within it. We have been influenced by the people and events in our lives and the culture in which we live. These influences blind us from a bigger understanding of who we are and what life is about. With our feet firmly cemented to the ground, our lives are always seen at eye level. We are stuck in a tunnel view rather than one that embraces the bigger perspective.

Once, while I was standing in the shade of a tree to watch my son's soccer game, a picture came into my mind and I received a message. The picture was of a circle, and I was standing on the edge of it. The message was, *Mary, you are standing outside of life.* I was shown and told that standing alone outside of the circle meant I was standing outside of God, which kept me separate from God. It was clear that I believed God was in one place and I was in another. It was as though God were begging me to step inside.

Step inside and live in me. The real life is in here, Mary. Don't stay on the outside. You got lost in the illusion of yourself. Let me absorb you back into me. I am the love. I am the life. I am the joy and the peace. Those words are the call for every one of us. *Let me absorb you* is the call to come home.

On our spiritual journeys, we must commit to being pursuers of wisdom and letting our experiences be catalysts for more learning rather than more ignoring. When life throws us a curve, we can learn to step into that circle for more wisdom. We can develop the willingness to learn, let go of ourselves, and embrace something outside of where our minds want us to stay. The intuitive inner source is always readily available if we are accessible and open to hearing it.

We have all been chosen and created to be an expression of God's imaginative power. We can only find that truth about ourselves when we are willing to let go of our preconceived notions of self-identity. Most importantly, we need to let go of the idea that we are separate from God and let him absorb us back into his life.

Practice

To begin your journey, sit quietly and breathe deeply. Let your body relax and center yourself in your heart. As openly and sincerely as you can, say (aloud or silently), "Show me who you are, who I am, and what I need to know." You will be heard, and your journey will begin, unfolding exactly as it has been designed, specifically for you.

CHAPTER ONE

Another View of Life

FACING MY BIGGEST FEAR, a fear of heights, I went skydiving one summer morning in Florida. We took off in a small propeller plane, and I watched as the ground got farther and farther away until we reached eleven thousand feet, our elevation for jumping. Tethered to a young man, I crawled with him to the door.

As I squatted in front of the open space, I asked myself and my buddy in tandem, "What the hell am I doing? I can't see anything, and we are jumping into thin air, for Pete's sake. How do we know the parachute will open?" I was giving up total control of my life, and I had never been so terrified.

"Are you ready?" he asked.

I took a deep breath and said, "No, but let's go." For the first minute and a half, we spun in circles at 120 mph. I thought it would never end. My brain was frozen, and I had no idea where my stomach was, but it was way beyond my throat. But the minute the cord was pulled, we slowed and stopped spinning, and our feet were aimed towards the ground. I could see the vastness of the land below.

It suddenly felt as if I were watching creation from a God's eye view. The breadth and beauty were endless.

From such a different vista, I calmly watched life taking place—houses, cars, streets, farms, all of it. A thought passed through my mind. *Look at creation, living life, covered in an umbrella of love.* And then one of my poems came to mind.

Sunshine

It's morning again; a new day is here,
The hours a gift of pure Love.
To walk in the light, with sunshine so bright,
Reflected on me from above.

As we floated to earth, my terror morphed into an all-consuming peace. I loved the view from above and beyond where we humans play out our lives. I saw only grace and joy. I was watching life below from a detached, observational point of view. There was nothing of the frenetic energy and stress generated when we can only see what is in front of our eyes. I had jumped over a cliff, as it were, and I was graced with a different view of all existence.

That is what the spiritual path is about. We trust and jump, and then we see life from a totally different point of view. We don't try to figure life out. We give ourselves over as we float through and embrace life as it comes to us and flows through us.

In Western culture, we are programmed to live by the values of logic, materialism, and accomplishments. Those values, added to that which we can perceive with our five senses, serve as our points of orientation. We ground ourselves in the physical and invest our truth in our mental abilities. In some cases, we move so far into logic to solve life's problems that we engage in simple, cold reasoning. We have been blinded by deeply engrained definitions of humanity, success, failure, and worth. We live in the head, not the heart and spirit. We don't jump and we don't let go. We plan, organize, and think it through.

When asked who we are, we answer from a perspective of life that is oriented around tangible realities. If we can touch and feel it or even label it, it is authentic. Culturally, we have been solidly planted in the left brain, which is the logical, sequential, verbal, linear, and analytical side of us. And when we alternate to the right brain, we become emotional about all the figuring out on the part of the left brain. This is how we relate to each other, events, and life itself, and it is how we find meaning and purpose. Logic has served as the basis for our education, both formal and informal, and it provides both method and content.

As a result of this orientation towards logic and the five senses, for many in our culture, spiritual explorations are relegated to hourly weekend events. And though our religious organizations take us beyond the tangibles, they are steeped in dogma. This puts a wall around what is perceived to be "truth" and rejects whatever is not contained within the box of specific doctrines. Anything outside that box is viewed as coming from some sinful source. These narrow religious opinions turn exploration into fear and stifle our right to expand our experiences.

The night before my mother died, she looked out into the room and said, "Oh, you are my sister. I want to go home." Her sister had died a few years earlier. Obviously seeing beyond the veil, my mother was being encouraged to take the next step.

I shared this anecdote with a fundamentally religious friend who immediately said that she didn't believe in such things. Yet, over and over, we hear stories of people on their deathbeds who experience something beyond themselves. It may be God as a dream or in a form that comes as comfort for making the transition.

When my grandmother was dying, she also spoke of what she saw. "The colors are so intense. It's the most beautiful place I've ever seen." The beauty was inviting her to step forward. It made me feel sad that my friend did not have the ability or desire to recognize the passageway between life here and life there. How many people are trapped in that same box? They won't open the door to a more expansive experience of life and God.

Rigid religious tenets prevent us from experiencing the fullness of life. Ideologies are formed when any one person or group begins to define God in a specific way or declare that their way is the only way. These rigid beliefs automatically create a box that becomes a spiritual coffin preventing further enlightened revelation. God cannot be confined. And wouldn't we all like to be comforted as we die—to say nothing of while we are living?

But because we value the objectively provable in our human lives and need the security of guidelines in our belief systems, we are not able to flow freely into the vastness of life, no matter where we look for answers. To find that vastness, we must choose or be drawn to the path beyond our human or ego-based selves. If we open to the path of awakening, the path opens. If we seek, the path never ends. When we are closed, the path is still there, but we are unable or unwilling to walk it.

Trying to embrace a specific definition of God—or the Universe, Life, Spirit, Essence, Divine Consciousness, Energy—is like believing that a single grain of sand can define the whole beach. Have you ever had an experience so grand that you didn't have words for it? It was just too big, deep, and incomprehensible for words. That is God. Words can't describe what Spirit is. To say that God is sitting on a throne in some formed place called heaven is a man-made assessment projected onto God. It's limiting. A god that is defined cannot be the true God. Humans don't have the capacity to know the whole of God.

I first got the concept of infinity as a little girl. Over and over, I played with it in my mind. *How can something be forever? How can it not end? But then, if there's a wall out there, what's on the other side of it?*

The Infinite cannot be explained. It is experienced. A spiritual journey is not about knowledge of God. It is about *experiencing* God. We must let go of what we believe and take the leap of faith to move forward, even at the risk of being struck by lightning. I say this from a place of experience, for I have jumped off the cliff and challenged the lightning.

The fundamentalist Baptist Church I attended for a few years when I lived in Atlanta had a very specific set of beliefs about God, as does almost every religious organization. Interestingly, there is no single unified definition of God within Christianity. Therefore, the so-called absolute truths are not absolute. If the truths were God-directed, they would be more consistent and not conflict with one another. It is not only arrogant to believe that one group has the real truth, it is as ignorant as supposing that the shade of blue we prefer is the only real blue.

After the service one Sunday, I was telling a friend that I questioned the validity of an entity called the devil. A church deacon overheard me, put his hand on my shoulder, and said, "If you don't believe in the devil, then you are not saved." With his hand still on me, he led me to the choir room and gently, but with determination, guided me to my knees to be saved.

The deacon's behavior is one example of the authoritarian beliefs and behaviors imposed by church members that pushed me to leave the rigidity of organized religion. Admittedly, it also didn't help that I'd been told men ruled over women, and because I was a woman, I could not teach Sunday School. This type of condescending behavior is certainly not the norm in all religious organizations, but by virtue of being "organized," rules in religion are always present in varying degrees.

When I finally rejected the God-box, I walked out of church, feeling betrayed and confused by those who were supposed to extend the love of God. As I walked to my car, I said, "If that's who you are, God, you can go to hell." I waited to be struck by lightning. Instead, a single, clear sentence drifted into my mind. *Good. Now I can show you who I really am.*

While exposure to spiritual beliefs is a great beginning on the journey with God, it is only a beginning. At that point, I was no longer willing to interpret the spirit or essence of God by external standards or by what anyone else said—even the great scholars. After all, everyone is subject to personal or political experience and biases, including academics and religious leaders. Instead, I listened to what was inside of me. I stated, "I ask that you, the Universe, be my guide, and I will know deeply in my heart that my direction and truth come from you." Leaving behind all other sources, I listened only to what I instinctively knew God was saying to me and through the core of my being. I had no agenda, no preconceived ideas, and no desire to confine God. I was open to letting Spirit be my teacher.

Incredible events emerged and characterized my journey. In surrendering to the pull of my heart rather than my mind, I learned to let go of the idea of a separate self. To get me there, all of my spiritual experiences have been required, however unwise, painful, immature, humorous, courageous, or mystical.

Both Eastern and Western religion support the concept that surrendering to the journey, surrendering to God, is necessary.

> *"If anyone would come after me, let him deny himself and take up his cross daily and follow me. For whoever would save his life will lose it, but whoever loses his life for my sake will save it."*
> (NIV, Matthew 16:24-25)

> *By letting it go, it all gets done. The world is won by those who let it go. But when you try and try, the world is beyond the winning.*
> (Lao Tzu)

> *In the end these things matter most:*
> *How well did you love? How fully did you love?*
> *How deeply did you learn to let go?*
> (The Buddha)

The bottom line is this: Give it up! The most important part of the journey to waking up is letting go. We have to jump out of the helicopter of our own beliefs to get a bigger, broader view. We have to let go of all we think is true, or have been taught is true, to let the Spirit of Life, rather than man, teach us. God cannot be defined or confined. We must go beyond the coffin of a belief system. Is that possible? Yes, if we are willing to jump into thin air and trust what happens.

Only when we are in the act of surrender, as one might do in the physical death process, can we see the connection between the world of our human senses and the one beyond the veil. Life is so much bigger with an all-encompassing view from which we can embrace a wisdom that never ends.

It was amazing to see life from a different perspective as happened when I jumped. As they were dying, two people I knew saw something that was not confined by human definitions. We make life too small. Jump out of a plane, seek beyond the veil, and be willing to be big.

Once, in a counseling session, I buried my head in my hands and cried, "I don't want to be that big." I was seeing that God wanted to take me somewhere much greater than where I was, and he wanted me to be someone much greater than who I was. It shocked me. It would require that I let go of all self-imposed limitations and all perceptions of myself to unleash the boundaries of who I could be. The thought of being that exposed terrified me.

To even begin touching the fullness of God and who we are as his creations, we must surrender everything about ourselves: our egos, ideas, perceptions, beliefs, and desires. We must also surrender any dogma, doctrine, or rules that tell us definitively who God is, what he wants, and how he behaves. When we are no longer stuck in our identities, concepts, or traditions, we are free to embrace a bigger truth.

Whom will we follow? Ourselves or our Selves?

> **Practice**
>
> Tap into all you believe about God and write it down. Do not just look at what you have learned about God (knowledge) but also at what you have experiened (revelation). Is God friendly, authoritarian, tangible, intangible? Does he speak to people, or is he silent? Is "he" a he, a she, or an it?
>
> Have you had a one-on-one experience with God? How did that make you feel? Consider the quality of the meeting. Were you challenged, comforted, or both? If you have not had such an experience and want one, ask for it. Ask God to show you something way beyond logic. If you want to get precise about it, ask for something specific about you or your life.

CHAPTER TWO

What Is Spirit and Who Am I?

So what is this thing called Spirit that we can turn to, depend upon, and let live and flow freely in us, as us?

The first words in the Bible are, "In the beginning, God . . . ." (NIV, Genesis 1:1) Everything that *is* came from God. All that exists is a manifested form of this act of creation. Nearly the same words are used in the Koran: "At the beginning, God created . . ." And the Tao Te Ching states, "In the beginning was the Tao and the Tao was with God and the Tao was God." God is our essence and we are individual forms of that essence.

Joel Goldsmith, author of a book entitled *The Infinite Way*, was a Jewish-Christian mystic, and his book came to me soon after I left organized religion, right on the heels of what God said to me on my way out through the parking lot. The timing was perfect.

One night after my kids were asleep, I was lying on my bed, reading a chapter about God as the Universal Consciousness. It was nothing like the God-in-the-sky of mainstream doctrine, but it was very much like what Jesus said: "The kingdom of God does not come with observation; nor will they say, 'See here!' or 'See there!' For indeed, the kingdom of God is within you." (NIV, Luke 17:20-21)

As I read Goldsmith's words about God being all of us, that idea jumped off the page, sinking deep into my heart, which then resonated with a very loud *Yes!*

You may have had a moment of sudden illumination like that in which you unexpectedly receive an epiphany, a point of light, a truth you didn't know before. Planted in your core, this concept comes alive with meaning. For me, this was not an intellectual understanding but struck me as an aha moment. Instantly, I knew that God was not "out there" in some place called heaven, nor could I possibly be separate from him because I had been created by and of him. Pure and simple. I understood that I didn't need to *try* to connect with God because I was already connected. It became obvious that I was and always had been part of him, an expression of Divine Consciousness, or God, which "in the beginning" created form.

I was floating on cloud nine and filled with love, in complete awe of the fact that I was actually part of God. But after the joy came the panic. Everything I thought I knew about God had been suddenly redefined. The shift was huge, and all I could think was *Oh no, I am going to hell now.* My mind had suddenly jumped in front of my beautiful vision and disturbed the peace, ranting at me, asking *What in the world are you thinking? This is blasphemy.* My mind tried to take away the wisdom and beauty I had been given.

The mind will constantly latch onto something to prevent enlightenment because new information always challenges old belief systems. But that's what growth is about. All at once you have an insight, and in that instant, you are separated from your old beliefs, your old self, and sometimes, all of your closest friends and relatives! The mind will try to undermine those insights to maintain the status quo.

This is how the spiritual journey to awakening will unfold. We keep seeing things that we didn't see or know before. When we've seen some truth, we can't un-see it. When it comes with a powerful *Yes!* we don't want to let it go. In fact, we want to help others see it too. But not everyone wants to hear it. They can't face things that would force them to change their minds. Yet resistance is what keeps us stuck in a box.

I was two-thirds of the way through a workshop I was conducting several years ago when I alluded to this concept that God is all of us. Since my audience shared mainstream beliefs, they agreed that God had created everything. I carried this belief further and urged that it is impossible to be separate from God's creation. I actually said, "The kingdom of God is within you."

Instantly, the energy of the group changed. The participants distanced their attention and some refused to look at me. When the program was over, one woman stood up, looked me in the face, and with great drama, threw her workbook in the trash. The next day, a different participant lashed out saying, "I don't even know if you are saved." These people seemed to be so stuck in their belief systems that they could not expand a single inch. And even though I cited a verse from their own Bible, I did so with a broader meaning than they could or would take in. Rigid beliefs form a coffin, housing corpses and killing free exploration or revelation.

The lesson is that rigidity thwarts the process of enlightenment. To allow for more enlightenment, we must always be willing to open the window a wee bit more, expand our views, and constantly change and redefine what we have previously held to be true. We can't get to the fifth grade and declare that we are now fully educated. We have to find the willingness to keep learning and seeing things from a slightly different view.

When I was getting my master's degree in adult education, we studied a book titled *The Courage to Teach*, by Parker Palmer. I found his views on openness and learning to be very inspiring. He believes that for students to learn deeply, they must understand the risks involved, but they must also feel safe. We can certainly think of students as being more than young people sitting in a classroom. We are all students of life. If we are on a spiritual path, we take the risk of waking up to discover that the truth is not what we once perceived. We are not separate from God. God is the core of our being and all that we are. That is where our safety lies.

Joel Goldsmith played a huge role on my journey to waking up. In the introduction to *The Infinite Way* he says this:

> The great Power necessary to dispel the erroneous conditions which surround us must be sought within ourselves. We are seeking, as never before, that which will free us from the fears, anxieties and dangers of material living. We know that whatever it is that will give us mental rest and spiritual peace does not lie in the realm of human thought.

We live under the illusion that material forces and human will are great powers, until we learn that within our own being there is a spiritual power, which dispels this illusion.

There is a "Peace, be still" within our own consciousness which will still every storm in our experience, heal our diseases, lift us above the strife and weariness of human existence.

Our part is to recognize its presence within ourselves and let it fulfill its mission.

What is Goldsmith saying? In simple terms he is recommending that we get out of the way. He is also saying that there is nothing we need to do to obtain the life of God within us; we just need to see or believe that we are that Life and surrender to it. Truth (peace, love, and life) is known in the heart, not the head. The thoughts of the mind are just that—puffs of air like clouds floating by. We can grab them or watch them.

In a letter to Helen Keller regarding her being accused of taking a story idea from someone else, Mark Twain said, "The kernel, the soul, let us go further and say the substance, the bulk, the actual and valuable material of all human utterances is plagiarism. For substantially all ideas are second-hand, consciously and unconsciously drawn from a million outside sources."

Consider these facts. Since the beginning of humanity, people have been thinking. They have had thoughts about everything from hunger to hatred versus love, beauty versus ugliness, and right versus wrong. Every subject on Earth has been felt, experienced, talked or written about, and analyzed to death. "What has been will be again, what has been done will be done again; there is nothing new under the sun." (NIV, Ecclesiastes 1:9)

Not one of our thoughts is original. That fact is disconcerting because it tends to make us feel so much less important. But it also helps us see that it is safe to let go of thoughts or beliefs because they have not originated with us. We can think, ponder, and worry until we exhaust ourselves, and it does no good. It's easy to let go of them when we see them for what they are. We can then trust the power that knows how to take care of everything and get out of our own way. But as long as we believe our thoughts, we suffer. As long as we believe that we are in control or even that we need to contribute, we struggle.

Once we wake up, everything shifts. What we *thought* of as our problems disappear. When we stop being confined, attacked, or tormented by our thoughts, all things begin to work together spontaneously. Life begins to flow by the nature of being free.

The spiritual journey is one of exploration and faith. Consider the difference between living in the stress of being good enough to meet the demands of doctrine or the fear of what might happen to us if we "go astray" and letting the pure essence of God live through us, without thought. Give the steering wheel to God and sit in the passenger seat. We can either live in fear, feeling a need to help the outcome of our lives, or we can live in peace knowing the life we live is God's life in us, as us. The fact is, we already have God's life within us. The issue is how to activate it.

Practice

Consider a deeply held belief that you have been forced to release. It could be about a person or situation. It could be about something you learned in a book or through experience. What forced you to let that belief go? Was it easy or hard? What were the benefits of changing your mind?

Did you ever believe something about God that later changed? Did you ever read a scripture one way and then see it in another? Are you willing to do that again? And again? And yes, again?

CHAPTER THREE

Getting on the Moving Sidewalk

HOW DO WE BEGIN A SPIRITUAL JOURNEY? It happens when we are willing to take a different path. We come to a fork in the road and choose a different direction from our former way.

We are spiritual beings in human form, having human experiences. When we open to it, God will use our human journey to wake us up. We are who we are—expressions of the Universe. We just became so mesmerized by the chaos and stress of the human life that we fell asleep, we forgot.

If we are willing, we can wake up and live in and as the peace beyond understanding. We will not only overcome the issues that concern us, we will not even notice them. But if we continue to live from the mind, we struggle and fight against what is happening and often feel defeated. Our minds taunt us: *Your life is a mess. You must do more. You'll never get it right. This is too hard.*

There were many times when I desperately sought answers to the problems in my life. My recourse was to pray, read, think, or consult with others while I waited for wisdom and answers. In other words, I worked at it. Then, once when I was seeking guidance, I was given a clear image that quickly condensed in my mind. It had nothing to do with finding answers. It was about stopping all effort to do so.

A moving sidewalk, much like the ones in airports, appeared in my mind. It wound its way through a park and continued into a field of trees, grass, and wildflowers. Next to the moving sidewalk was a paved path similar to a walking trail. With the picture came a direct statement: *Mary, you can get on and move effortlessly with the flow or you can run alongside, trying to keep up living under your own power.*

Not being much of a runner, the choice was easy. I had to get on and ride. Of course, I often got off the moving sidewalk and began running again. This dance between ease and self-effort would happen when life threw hard challenges at me. I would run like an Olympian, trying to fix problems until my heart pounded and I lost my breath. Only in complete exhaustion did I finally learn to quit. Worn out, I would think: *Oh wait . . . fixing that problem is not my job! Get back on the moving sidewalk, Mary, and let it be done by God. After all, it's not my life; I have been created to let him flow through me.*

To get on that moving sidewalk and let God do the living, there are things we must do and understand. One is to see ourselves as clearly as possible. We need to get rid of beliefs we have acquired about ourselves that are no longer true or never were true.

Second, we must heal ourselves from the wounds caused by outmoded messages and experiences. We've all been hurt in varying degrees. It's the nature of the human journey. These imbedded pains or misperceptions can be something that happened in our communities, schools, or within our own families. For example, someone who desperately wanted to act might not have been chosen for a role in the school play. Because they were not chosen, they might have felt rejected and that they weren't good enough. The reality might have been more benign: The part that would have been theirs might have been cut. The perception of unworthiness—of not being good enough—stays with them, though it shouldn't, and they cling to a self-judgment they made long ago.

The bottom line is that we need to heal the ego-self so we can comfortably let it go. And the reason for healing ourselves is that we are so deeply rooted in our stories that we cannot move until we feel good enough to release them. If they are not released, they will continually pull us back into the feelings and beliefs of a personal self because our stories have fabricated our mis-identity. We need to understand that we are not separate from Creation. When we see separation as an illusion, we are able to understand why we have been so desperate to find our Source. We realize we have been seeking comfort from the pain caused by the feeling of separation.

Albert Einstein believed that we are part of a whole, the Universe, but we have deluded ourselves into believing we are separate from everything else and that this delusion is a prison. Because I am a visual person, I often see lessons as pictures. Regarding the "whole" Einstein referred to, a picture came to me of a pot of boiling water, which was the Whole. From it bubbles popped up, which were different forms or manifestations of the Whole. In that image, one bubble is you, one is me, one is the rose bush, another is the family pet. All life comes from one source. The water forms bubbles and materializes as separate, but they are not. They are the same thing in different forms.

Putting our worth in self-perception and cultural values, we live by conditioned patterns, and we are frequently triggered by emotions attached to past events that taint our present situations and become a burden. Who doesn't get tired of feeling that they aren't enough? We see and feel ourselves as the image of experiences or as others have painted us to be, but we do not need to be prisoners of external perceptions, whether those of our parents, friends, teachers, coworkers, spouses, or even children.

We are not created to be defined by the human world, nor are we created to be just a human self. We must wake up and learn that we have never been and cannot be separate from the Life that created us. We are specific expressions of a Divine Consciousness. Nothing less; nothing more.

When I was in my late thirties, I had a very unusual experience, showing me exactly who I was created to be. The experience didn't change my journey, but it gave me a big piece of the puzzle about God being my source and that, as Dannion Brinkley said, you were chosen to come here. I was being counseled by two lovely Christian ladies who were willing to seek God's healing in a variety of ways. On one occasion, they asked, "Would you like to look at your life and find out where you feel stuck?" I nodded. Of course, I was willing. I was willing to do anything to heal the accumulated pain of my experiences.

As we sat in a dimly lit, quiet room, they assured me that from the beginning of my life and through all of my struggles, God had always been with me. They wanted me to know that no matter how hard things had been, I had never been alone. They asked Spirit to guide us, and I closed my eyes as we began to look back on my life.

Following their words, I envisioned my life, going backwards in time. I saw myself in my twenties, as a teen, and as a young child. In my mind, I could see myself at each stage. I was a fully grown but not worldly young adult. I was blossoming into a woman as a teen. Then I saw the tall, skinny tomboy I was as a child. I was instructed to feel myself at those ages. "Feel your heart and your stomach and any other sensation." Nothing nudged at me. I was only aware that I had felt lonely and lost all that time.

They continued, taking me back to the age of ten, the age of six, and when I was a toddler. Nothing happened of any consequence except a feeling of deep loneliness. "Let's go back to you being an infant." Nothing. "Now you are in the womb." Nothing. "Let's go back to your creation."

As one of them spoke of my beginning, when the egg and sperm merged, I jumped. I suddenly saw a golden ray of light and heard myself with unbounded enthusiasm exclaim, "I'm alive! I'm alive!" I began to travel down a softly glowing tunnel, and with great passion, I spoke with God about the joy of having life.

Though he had no form or voice, I was bathed in his presence. He was the golden light in which I was created and now moved. His eye was fully upon me, and I felt the love of a smile unseen. Our shared joy was that I was to become his expression in human form. I was everything he was, beginning to take form and enter his world.

In that beautiful experience, I understood that I could never be alone because the essence of life was not just in me, it *was* me. God had given himself form, and as that form, I was an expression of him. As God's form, I would be going into the world for a purpose. We would never be apart, and I would always be protected and loved as I was in that moment of entering the world. I saw that the journey would be hard and at times dark, but I wasn't going alone.

Just as all humans do, I had lost that connection because I had been trained to embrace my form as my identity. I fell asleep to the meaning and purpose of who I am once I suffered the limitations of humanity. And even when I had that experience, I didn't understand its full significance because I was still too attached to my personality and believed so strongly in what I had experienced in life. I saw truth, yet I remained asleep.

The journey to awakening is about remembering who we are. It would be many, many years before I could put all the pieces together and fully remember who I am. But I was blessed to be on the way. We will not be able to live freely if we believe simultaneously that our humanity has a personal identity and that we are flowing in the love and grace of who we really are. We cannot be two in one—humanity and spiritual flow. Only when we liberate ourselves from our self-identity can we be free.

When one of my closest friends died, I knew her essence was somewhere in the universe, but I wanted to know more. As I was driving home from the grocery store that June day, I asked, "Where are you?" Looking out the car window, I saw a beautiful blue sky filled with billowy clouds, and placed upon it was a white envelope. The ends of the envelope were slit open, and I saw my friend as the God-essence, moving from the fullness of the sky to enter the envelope and manifest as Shirley for seventy-eight years. When that manifestation was finished, she moved out of the envelope and merged back into the One energy of the sky. She came as Energy, or God, to live in form as Shirley, and she left to be creative Energy again. She is still here, but simply no longer visible as a unique human manifestation.

It is our purpose to be as free and flowing as the life of my friend that I glimpsed through this image. We can just enjoy the envelope of expression and be who we are rather than being weighed down by our need for a personal identity and the struggle to manipulate or control how life plays out for us. We are meant to be open, letting life flow, and to live as spiritual beings having a human experience.

In the Bible, Jesus says, "Therefore, I tell you, do not worry about your life, what you will eat or drink; or about your body, what you will wear. Look at the birds of the air; they do not sow or reap or store away in barns, and yet your heavenly Father feeds them. Are you not much more valuable than they?" (NIV, Matthew 6:25-26)

We are not meant to figure out life as though it were ours. We are meant to enjoy life as it unfolds before us and through us. We have all been created in the same light and we all floated down the tunnel of love. We were created to be an expression in form. We have the right and the obligation to get out of the way, stop human effort, get on the moving sidewalk, and let life move us forward.

Picture being in a pool of water and putting your arms in front of you, floating with your hands open, making no effort. It's restful and easy. Until we relax, get out of the way, let go of our own agendas, and stop trying to determine what it all means, we will not find that kind of freedom.

We have been put to sleep by the experience of life, and we must understand how the sleep happened so we can wake up. No matter what the belief system, our great spiritual leaders of the past all had to wake up: Moses on the mountain, Jesus in the desert, and Buddha under the bodhi tree.

When we understand that we are the light of God in human form, as I saw myself in the womb, we flow . . . and glow! When we stop trying to steer our own course, life unfolds and all our heavy baggage falls away. It becomes easy when we can get on the moving sidewalk and let life take us where it will. We are then able to use our human experiences to heal and transform ourselves, to become less and less attached to our identity as a personal and separate self, and to open to being the God that is in us and expressed as us. We can be our unique selves without the burdens and misperceptions we accumulate when we think we are separate or in control. We begin to live as we were meant to live, fully and freely, when we get on that moving sidewalk.

Practice

This one is simple, but it may be scary. Open your heart and say, "I want to be who I was created to be. Put me on the path."

Chapter Four

Doing Versus Being

SINCE THE BEGINNING OF TIME, human existence has been about physical reality. But we have moved beyond the mere struggle to survive, and we now subsist by guidelines, values, and beliefs to direct us. All of these things help us live our lives and form who we think we are.

As a society and culture, we cannot live without a sense of self-worth. We try to find it in what we do. We live in the pursuit of things that afford us power or are symbols of power, be they money, titles, homes, clothes, or friends. To do this, we live by rules that are logical, rational, and confined to the arena of the mind. As a society and culture, we perceive things in concrete and material terms.

We have formed opinions and judgments about beauty, intellect, and supremacy, and we believe our own definitions about significance. We inhabit a culture of comparison, and we identify ourselves by what we do or have done, rather than by who we actually are.

Think about the all-important elevator speech. In thirty seconds, we learn to share a clear, brief message about who we are, what we do, what we desire, and how we can be of benefit. Is that all we are? An elevator speech?

When people are asked to define themselves, they usually begin with words that tell what they do. "I am a nurse." "I am a banker." "I am a gardener." "I am a travel agent." None of these answers relay who we are. They are all just roles we play. Who we are and what we do are not the same, yet we define ourselves by our activities. We are enmeshed in what we do—and our thoughts, feelings, and experiences revolve around that function. We focus our attention and expend our energy on an identity of doing.

As we grow up, we develop a sense of self-identity by conforming to certain beliefs, behaviors, and goals. We have been labeled by experiences and people, which then lead us to create definitions for the identity of the ego-self. When we mature, we fall into even deeper definitions of who we are or who we should be, and our ego begins to conform to those definitions. Importance is all about what we do—or don't do—in our human lives. We put our human "doing" on center stage and wear an appropriate costume as though we were that character. While performing that role, we stress over our performance. "What if I'm not the best at my job?" "What if I fail as a boss?" "What if people don't like what I do?" "If I earn money and accolades, I'll be successful. If I don't, I'll be a failure."

Our roles and jobs, fulfilling or not, are limiting. When we define ourselves by what we do, whatever the role, we open ourselves to comparisons, which then lead to judgments. "Sam is a good actor, but he's not as outstanding as Clare." If you are Sam, your ego feels bad. If you are Clare, your ego is soothed.

If we consider all the labels used to categorize people, we can see how they impact self-worth. Such labels create unhealthy comparisons and divisions, fueling insecurity, negativity, feelings of failure, and intense stress. Making labels significant can also make us feel defeated and even like victims. If we are not able to do what we believe marks us as successful or of value in the world, we can feel less important than others we perceive to be successful.

The fact is that no matter what we do, we derive automatic value from being a unique expression of God. Because of our intrinsic value, there can be no comparisons between us. The value of just *being* speaks to our worth. Should we chop down the trees in winter because they aren't producing leaves? From the outside, the trees are just being, not producing. On the inside, there is tremendous value in what will soon come forth.

Many years ago, I wrote a poem that speaks to the wonder of creation and the many ways in which God finds expression. The line about flakes of snow speaks to the beauty of each of us.

Winter Storm

Who can stand in the middle of a snowstorm
And deny there is a God
As the overwhelming sheet of white
Begins to cover the earth?

Who can watch the trees become statues,
Hands reaching to the sky,
And say the world does not sing
The praises of its Creator?

> Who can examine each intricate lacey flake—
> No two the same in form—
> And say it happened all by chance
> Without the perfect plan?
> Not I.

God expresses himself in an infinite number of forms. How can he not? Infinity is endless and expanding. Some people have considerable physical talents or looks, and others do not. Yet they are still equal as individual expressions of God's different forms. Some are quiet, spiritual, and deep. Others just love to live on the surface and play. Some are creative, expressive, and communicative. Others are introspective and introverts. Some are weak, and others are strong. Some feel deeply and are slow to speak. Others feel deeply but are quick to express themselves. Others are clever, quick, or highly intelligent, and some are simply quiet. We are infinite in variety.

Our bodies or minds are not the same, nor are our personalities. None of us can do exactly what another can do. As humans, we use comparisons and labels to demarcate what we consider to be the privileged and underprivileged, the beautiful and homely, the intelligent and unintelligent. These descriptions seem to define who we are, yet they have nothing to do with the value bestowed by the Universe.

I was always told by my parents that I was attractive and intelligent. Sounds good, doesn't it? Not so much. My parents were biased, so that colored the assessment. And those labels became my sole identity, all I thought I had. I was never told that I was kind, loving, interesting, fun, good, or wise. So I perceived that I had none of those qualities. I was only of value for a body I didn't create and a brain that I was given by virtue of genetics.

Using the human definition of value, we are also prone to dig into the mire of trying to fix inequalities. We grieve about perceived unfairness and act without understanding that there is nothing to fix. In the essence of being a creation of God, there is no inequality and there is no lack. Lack or its opposite, abundance, are perceptions on the human plane. Most important is the fact that each perceived form of lack is an opportunity to reach inward.

There have been times in my life when I lived in dire financial circumstances. And while that was very painful, it was also what prompted me to seek answers from a spiritual source. Had life been comfortable, I would never have pursued anything but the values of our culture. In retrospect, I see that having no one to rescue or help me was the perfect plan for the unfolding of my spiritual awakening. And I'm thankful for that because rescue would have interfered with the divine plan.

Each divine creation has its purpose. Each situation has its purpose. But we demean what the Universe has chosen as its expression by thinking a person without the high intellect, a high paying job, or a beautiful body is less than someone who has one or more of those things. There is no difference between a rose and a dandelion. The values established in our human system are shallow and untrue.

We also negate what God is doing through each person when we feel a need to rescue someone or some group. My first understanding of this came when I realized that someone had to play Judas. Jesus' sacrifice on the cross had to be set up by someone walking Earth at the same place and time. We often have so little ability to see the big picture. Look at the history of civilization. We are basically the same people with the same conflicts and issues. We need to stop trying to fix the world. Our purpose is to fix ourselves. When we do that, we automatically begin to fix the world. When *we* improve, everything around us improves. Change comes on an individual basis.

My father would have been called privileged, yet when he was in his late eighties, he had dementia. All that drive, education, prestige, and money no longer mattered. In fact, with dementia and the loss of his thinking ability, he became relaxed, unaware of himself, quiet, and easy. Without socially imposed standards for success, he was free to just be. We can all be that free and still have our minds in working order.

To see who we are more clearly, we must look at the meaning of *doing* versus *being*. The definition of *doing* is to perform, act, execute, exert, produce, and carry out. All of these are actions, things to be accomplished, and they have a beginning and an ending. All of us have lived or are living in the "doing" of life. We get up, go to work, focus on the issues at hand, go to happy hour or the gym at the end of the day, go home to bed, and then do it all again.

The definition of *being* is to exist, have reality, breathe, live, remain undisturbed or constant, and to abide. All of these words imply a passive state, one that is already accomplished, one with no judgment, and this state is just to exist as it is.

In my life, the state of being has been something I've grown into. But the ego kept looking for meaning, at least in little remnants. Retired and single, it was sometimes especially challenging to live while having no agenda. I felt worthless just sitting on the sofa, reading or watching a snowstorm. There seemed to be no purpose to my life because I had no pressure to "do." The truth is that there is nothing for the ego to do once we wake up.

Upon awakening, doing is gone and our existence is our purpose. That bears repeating: Our existence is our purpose. We are created in unique form with unique traits, and they will be used. Being is not a call to just sit around. Our days will unfold naturally. We will create spontaneously. We will feel motivated from within to produce and act. Life lives itself according to what it wants to do.

One time I had a plan to visit a friend on a Monday. My goal was to clean house on Saturday, pack on Sunday, and leave on Monday. As it turned out, on Friday I noticed my bedroom blinds were dusty and got a cloth to wipe them off. Without thinking or planning it, I ended up cleaning the entire house on Friday instead of Saturday. I packed up Saturday morning and left for my friend's house on Saturday afternoon. Life was living its plan through me. I knew that and just let it flow. As it turned out, another friend showed up on Saturday, and I would have missed the mini-reunion had I left on my schedule.

Our obsessive need for doing comes from the ego striving for order and worth. I believe that in the process of falling asleep to who we really are, we feel lost and cannot ground ourselves. We desperately try to find meaning, and in the process of searching for that meaning we substitute doing for being. As long as we tie our worth to our doing, we will not let go. Yet once we are out of the way, God will live more fully through us. Once all traces of my "self" got out of the way, I found myself living more from my true self, my true nature. I was writing, feeling love (inside and out), and bringing joy to people. I didn't work at it. Fullness just began to happen.

God can fulfill his purpose once we get out of the way. Our bodies will be taken care of, our thoughts will be directed, our lives will be lived, and our joy will be overflowing. Our goal must be to find our value in being expressions of the Universe and knowing that what we are is already perfect, even in our imperfection. We start by understanding how our body, mind, and spirit work together.

Take a look at the world today. We strive intensely. We live in more doing and even less relaxing than ever before. Children can't or don't go outside to play, so they are not renewed by nature. They too are indoctrinated early by all the extracurricular activities in which they are involved. How many dance classes, soccer camps, guitar lessons, and baseball teams do they need? Yes, even our children cannot relax and just enjoy being—even through play. They don't have a chance to connect with their inner self. Being part of a tennis team may seem like play, but the underlying goal is to win. Is there something wrong with winning? No, of course not—unless it becomes what we most value about playing instead of valuing the fun of being your best.

And how many adults just go for a leisurely walk, skip a rock over water, sit outside and absorb the sun, or otherwise truly play? Adults also identify play with accomplishing something: going to the gym as a part of maintaining health, playing golf to get better at it, reading a book to enhance our education, or participating in happy hour to socially connect. All of these are good things to do, but perhaps the real question for ourselves is one of motivation. Why are we doing what we do?

Competition, division, and resentment are at an all-time high. Rather than coming together, we are feeling more separation. When we define life by doing to increase socially and culturally valued accomplishments and possessions, we are automatically put on the stress-train. And that train goes faster and faster the more we feel a need for success via labels. Such pressure cannot be sustained. We will implode, crash and burn, or die.

The good news is that it can all come to an end by seeing who we really are, not identifying with who we try so hard to be.

Practice

Before considering *doing* versus *being*, what was your elevator speech, or if you don't have one, what would it have been? Who were you? What did you want in life? Why were you important? Now, create a new elevator speech for yourself as Spirit *being*—apart from the doing.

CHAPTER FIVE

Connecting Body, Mind, and Spirit

WHEN WE SEE OURSELVES AS A WHOLE that functions in flow, we move one step closer to an understanding that we have been formed by the Universe. Just as God's universe functions in harmony, so can we. That whole is actually a triune comprised of body, mind, and spirit. Seeing ourselves as that combined and connected threesome puts us in balance and harmony. We no longer see our bodies as who we are from the outside. We no longer see our minds as the instruments for what we can do, accomplish, or believe. And we no longer see our spirit as disconnected from the "human" parts of us. Each part of our triune being works with the others and has a purpose.

The body relates and reacts to our physical environment. It allows us to move within time and space. Our bodies also express emotions. Who hasn't seen anger in a person's face or felt the pain of loss in their stomach? The body is also a doer. It eats, sleeps, walks, exercises, turns on the TV, goes to work, and plays games on the phone.

The mind is comprised of the intellect, will, and feelings. The thoughts of the mind trigger our emotions and actions in relation to others or situations we are in. The mind positions itself as if it were our self, and it takes over. It is also the judge of life, and we have fallen prey to believing what it tells us. Like the body, the mind is a doer. It evaluates, judges, speaks, and thinks in response to what is going on in the world around it. It also partakes in playing games on the phone!

The Spirit is the life of our being. It is the part of us that functions with wisdom, detached observation, and intuition. The Spirit is peace, and it loves unconditionally. Spirit is the substance of our manifested beings, and without it, we cannot exist. We often think that when the body dies, the Spirit leaves. It is actually the opposite: When the Spirit leaves, the body dies.

Each of our triune parts is interconnected and interacts with the others, and we are a bit like a volcano. On the outside can be seen form (the body). On the inside is heat (the mind) and at the core is energy (Spirit) that expresses through it.

The body is the form through which the essence of life is expressed. We *use* it, but we do not *own* it. We need to stop saying, "My body . . ." because we rarely add "is beautiful" or "feels great." We usually add something in the form of a complaint.

The mind is a tool for interacting with the world, but it is not our identity. As with the body, we need to catch ourselves in the act of saying, "I think . . ." or "I feel . . ." and stop. The mind's thoughts trap us in human experience and limit us to what we perceive. In an interview, author and awakened teacher Eckhart Tolle commented that he uses his mind when he engages with other people but doesn't live from his mind. Not letting the mind be in control is a learning process.

Spirit is the source from which we are meant to live. When we do that, the body and mind come into harmony, and we are not harnessed by what the world says and does or what we feel and think. In one of my favorite books, *Silence of the Heart* by Robert Adams, the author tells us that there is a power that knows how to take care of everything and will take care of your body—if you stop thinking. That's a powerful statement.

Rather than being separate, when Spirit is in control, the body and mind become connected vessels. They (body and mind) help each other. We can relate what we think to how we feel or we can relate the information coming from how we feel to what we think. And when Spirit is what pours through our veins and heals our bodies, we feel that as well. Spirit also fills our thoughts and calms our minds.

When we stop living from the idea of a separate self but know through experience the mind and body are tools through which the Spirit lives, stress disappears. We no longer feel the need to be in control of life or its outcomes, and we begin to pay attention to our bodies rather than just using them. Most importantly, we disengage from the chaos of human behavior and simply watch life unfold.

Practice

What are you thinking about your body right now? Write down what is going on and what you need to do. Now ask your spirit what it wants to tell you about your body. Are they the same?

Now be aware of what you are thinking. What thoughts keep running through your mind? Are they positive or negative? Do they trap you in a place of wanting or a place of judging? Ask spirit to clearly show you what thoughts are keeping you trapped.

CHAPTER SIX

The Body

SCIENTIFICALLY, BODIES ARE MASSES OF ENERGY in which each atom is individual and separate from the next. That is, while atoms physically influence one another, they never actually physically touch in the body. Molecules are even more separate, and if we go far enough into the mass of energy that is the body, we eventually arrive at simply a lot of open space. In other words, we are basically hollow. This is another way to understand that we are just a part of this great big universe of energy.

So what do our bodies do? A lot. They house, sustain, and warn us. They give us mobility and carry out the orders of the mind and Spirit. They can also speak to us about what is happening in parts of us, which means we can learn to listen to how our thoughts impact how we feel physically. We can also gain answers and wisdom from the body's connection to the Spirit within.

In truth, our bodies contain mystical energy that helps connect us to our spirits, aids us in our awakening, and guides us on our spiritual paths. Our bodies contain great wisdom in the cells, which contain memories and emotions that can inform us about our journeys. By listening to our bodies and the memories contained within our cells, we can heal both physically and psychologically.

Other than focusing on our external appearance, we give our bodies little attention—or at least not until they are not behaving as we would like them to. And yet, we are deeply identified with them. They present us to the world, and we often connect with others on the basis of looks, fashion, or athletic ability. How our bodies appear on the outside is at the forefront of our minds.

In our culture, we are very concerned with the body's appearance. We complain about the hips, the waist, the wrinkles, and the sagging muscles. The nose is too big; the lips are too small. The hair is too thick or thin. We also get caught up in body worship. *People Magazine* devotes an issue each year to the fifty most beautiful people—and they aren't talking about inner beauty. In reality, we have little control over the basic bodies we are given. We get what is in the gene pool. But our bodies are the envelopes of our expression of Spirit as form. They are not us.

Our bodies can also speak to us about other things. Stress-induced headaches, gut issues, a stiff neck, and fatigue are just a few body issues that can be linked to thoughts and feelings. The body's connection with our thoughts and feelings indicates that the body not only functions as a place to be but also serves as a system of signals or warnings, alerting us that we need to fix something in our lives.

The most common reaction to problems in our bodies is to reach for a cure. It's the bandage of choice for whatever we are suffering from in the physical realm. We want an aspirin for a headache. We want an antacid for the tummy. We want sleeping pills when we can't sleep.

Rather than immediately reaching for a physical cure, we can pause and ask what the pain is telling us. In his book *Seeker of Visions*, Native American teacher Lame Deer advised that Westerners have forgotten this.

A while ago, I had an earache. I hadn't had one since childhood, and having one as an adult baffled me. I was learning the practice of listening to my body rather than trying to quiet its message with medicine. Spiritually, I knew that the earache meant that I didn't want to hear something, so I asked what I didn't want to hear.

When I got quiet, the answer came to me. I was tired of hearing my own stressful thoughts. I understood the message: Move on from that project and lighten the load. Mentally, I knew that was true, but my body was showing me as well. As soon as I unloaded the project and felt great emotional relief, the earache went away. I am not advocating against medical treatment in our lives. I am advocating that we look at physical issues from a variety of perspectives.

Listening to our bodies is one of the choices we make as we move more deeply into our spiritual journeys. We come to understand that our minds or logic alone cannot solve our problems. We can learn to pay attention to the implications of the mind-body connection, which can then inform us about our beliefs. Our bodies can help us make the right choices.

The body can provide a warning signal when we need to change a habit, let go of a relationship, quit a job, or release trapped emotions. And sometimes, it lets us know that we are doing the right thing because we feel peaceful. The body-mind connection is powerful.

Louise Hay was the author of *Heal Your Body* and the founder of Hay House, a mind-body-spirit publishing company, and she had a powerful personal story about how emotions and thoughts that lie within us are related to illness. Louise was raped when she was five years old, and as an adult, she was diagnosed with vaginal cancer. Rather than immediately having surgery, she bargained with her doctors to see if she could make a mind-body connection about the disease and try to heal it.

Louise believed that her cancer came from an attitude of deep resentment that was eating away at her body. She immediately began to work with a counselor on her resentment. She also worked on nutrition to detoxify her body and clear the stuck emotions. The third thing she did was to forgive. Several months later, she went in to be examined, and the cancer could not be found.

It only makes sense that since all parts of us are connected, they all take part in whatever may be our issues. Therefore, all parts of us can cooperate to make the problem go away as well. In *Heal Your Body*, Louise Hay outlined some of the physical issues that might be caused by particular thoughts and emotions. It is a great guidebook for becoming more adept at sorting out the mind-body connection, but it is only a guidebook. Just as I went inside to discern where my earache was coming from, so can you delve within to discover what your body is trying to tell you.

Even as we work with the connection between body and mind, we need to understand the bottom line. The body has been created as the vehicle through which the Universe manifests itself. God is here to enjoy life as, and through, all of its various vessels. Who or what grows the grapes on the vine? Who or what gives the bird supplies to build its nest? God made the vehicle and he will make sure it runs. Once we get rid of all the things that are in the way, Source will do very well on its own.

Practice

Sit quietly, place your hands in your lap, close your eyes, calm your mind, and breathe. Pay attention and feel what you are experiencing in your body. Feel and focus on any pain. Really go into it and ask what it wants you to know. What is the pain saying to you? What is the deeper message beyond just stress, anger, or depression? Ask if there is a lesson in the pain.

Then envision your body as an empty vessel through which the divine flows. You get out of the way and picture it as perfect.

CHAPTER SEVEN

The Mind

OUR MINDS CONTROL US more than anything else. We are captured by endless thoughts and chatter. Minds absorb and interpret the world. Our minds form ideas, interpret events, interact with others, respond to situations, and express emotions without our conscious input. Our minds translate everything for us. I guess we could say that we involuntarily let our minds be in control of our lives.

Sit still and close your eyes. Most likely your mind is wondering why I have asked you to do this. It is creating a thought around a question: *Why am I doing this?* Now ask yourself where your mind is located. Where did that thought in the form of a question come from? Where is the mind that gave birth to that thought?

If we try to locate the mind, we can't. It's like trying to define the shoreline. Is it the water or the beach? Is the mind the brain or the concepts it conjures up? Neurons are cells in the brain, but the thoughts that come forth are not tangible. In fact, because we have the ability to sit quietly, breathe deeply, and quiet ourselves, we can make the thoughts stop. We can also count on them to come back and interrupt the quiet. Thoughts are not us. They come and go, and we can take them in or watch them without owning them.

According to a National Science Foundation estimate, humans have between twelve thousand and sixty thousand thoughts a day. And they say that some experts estimate it is more like sixty thousand to eighty thousand thoughts a day, which is an average of twenty-five hundred to thirty-three hundred thoughts per hour. No matter how many thoughts I have, my mind won't even get around those statistics! It feels too crowded, too overwhelming, and impossible. When the National Science Foundation first came out with its own estimate, they also estimated that 80 percent of those thoughts are negative and 95 percent are repetitive. When I realize I am catching thought-balls all day long, it seems so unkind to myself. Why would I wear myself out like that?

When I am quiet, I see thoughts as clouds floating by. I can either grab the clouds or let them keep going. The grabbing is where we get in trouble because we aren't very selective. It's like being really hungry. We eat anything. The mind is always hungry to be busy, and it will grab whatever thought floats by.

Who and what feeds the mind? What gives it the nutrition to work so hard? Who and what are the people, events, and situations that trigger our minds into becoming walking encyclopedias that define everything? We might call the mind our computer and the information it holds our Google. Because it is the encyclopedia for our lives, everything that happens to us is catalogued within it. We can *consciously* search it when we want to know something, but *subconsciously*, we hear from it all the time.

Many of the stimuli that inform us take place in the moment, while other stimuli come from experiences accumulated throughout our lifetimes. The fact that we have received, interpreted, and retained information for as many years as we are old means that some of it is outdated, and some of it serves us well and some does not. Some of this information is correct and some is not. Some of it feels good and some is painful. Yet we unknowingly keep and use all those mental files, so while we exist in the present, we are guided by the past. And too often, suffering is caused by what happened in the past and/or our interpretations of it. We all have something that happened in our past that formed painful beliefs we have brought into the present.

Our parents play the first big role in forming our mind-based perceptions and thoughts because they are the ones with whom we have our first relationship. Parents create the input and foundation for our identity, who we think we are, and who we eventually will become—unless we change the lens of our perception.

Unfortunately, in many cases the lens we got from our parents is painful. Like contact lenses, they scratch and itch. They don't fit, and worse, they blur our vision. Consider an event in the life of a child that may have formed a negative feeling. Maybe a parent yelled at or blamed a child for something he didn't do. The parent punished the child, and he didn't understand why. But until we are willing to examine the impact of those events, we suffer the discomfort of the consequent negativity.

Our teachers and peers also impact us. They can be either kind or critical, and they make a huge impression when we are young. Events make an impact too: birth or death; winning an award or losing a game; moving to a new place or staying where we are. The ordinary events of life shape our sense of it, as well as the financial, geographical, and social situations in which we live.

As a young girl, my family lived in a small neighborhood where families knew each other, people waved and said hi, and the kids all played together. When I was six, we moved to a much larger house in an affluent neighborhood made up of older people. They were busy with their lives and did not mingle in warm or welcoming ways. As a child, I concluded that when people have money, they are self-absorbed and not as friendly. I made a gross generalization born of a six-year-old's comparisons.

Once I became willing to dig into my feelings and perceptions, I saw that I had defined myself by the judgments and views my parents imparted. I had buried many traumatic childhood events, which had created distorted views about my worth, the judgments of adults, and what love meant. I carried those errant and unhealthy beliefs until I had the courage to examine them.

As hard as it is, we must release the pain we carry. But we often bury events and feelings that are too overwhelming for us, and it is not like burial in the ground. The things buried within us cause us to view ourselves in false ways and have the potential to harm us physically, mentally, and emotionally.

One of the memories I was able to release had given me the deep belief that I had no value and should not be alive. Before I even uncovered this memory, I once told a friend, "I don't know what it is, but I feel like I am an inherently bad person." As an adult, I was carrying childhood perceptions and defining myself based on them without knowing it. The truth is that what upsets us is never what we think it is. Instead, what we think is the source of our pain is almost always connected to a deeper picture.

As a four-year-old, I was told by my mother to stay in the kitchen while she went to the basement. Wanting to have fun, I sneaked down the stairs to play peak-a-boo, but stopped at the bottom when I found her doing something she absolutely did not want me to see. She was horrified and enraged as she pulled me from the steps and out in front of her.

Pointing her finger and shaking her red-painted nail at me, she said in anger, "You are bad. You are very, very bad." She grabbed my hand, moved me to the corner of the basement, opened the door, and locked me in the coal cellar—the room used to store coal when there was a coal-burning furnace in the house. The small, dark room was musty and filled with junk. I sat on a dusty, rolled-up rug and hugged my knees.

Only after I heard her leave did the shock set in. But it was neither the coal cellar nor the anger I'd seen in my mother's face that terrified me. It was not even my own fear, which sat as a weight in my stomach. What terrorized me was being alive. At four years of age, I could not comprehend how to reconcile my existence with my mother's words that I was very, very bad. I was consumed by a question I could not answer. *If I am so bad, why am I alive?*

When input is traumatic, the reaction is raw emotion that embeds itself in the psyche. I suddenly "realized" that

I should not be alive. Most harmful experiences implant themselves in our minds and become part of who we perceive ourselves to be. These embedded negative interpretations are not true, and we must dig them out to find the truth of who we are so we can heal and move on.

Our minds also don't correctly discern the source of the information received. In my case, one source was my mother's humiliation and anger. Minds just take in experiences and form labels, which we attach to our ego-selves and our sense of self-worth. When our sense of importance is low or we feel defeated or bad, we often try to build ourselves up. We want to feel good whenever we can, even if it's just about something small. We live in a dance of ego-demeaning or ego-building situations. But we must stop the two-step by ridding ourselves of false perceptions and cover-up behaviors.

The truth is that we are not who someone else might say we are, nor are we defined by any of the experiences we have had. We are amazing, wonderful, valuable expressions and are loved deeply by the Divine Consciousness that created us out of its own essence. All of that love, peace, and sense of worth awaits us when we shed the illusion of a separate self and the damage connected with it.

Practice

Explore one painful experience from your childhood. What did you believe about the experience, the other people involved in it, and about yourself? Are these things true?

CHAPTER EIGHT

Mind-Based Beliefs

WE CANNOT SEE THE TRUTH until we are willing to see the lie. The truth is that there is only Source. The lie is that there is a self. We will never let go of the sense of self that we have developed and cling to until we are willing to see that it is all an illusion of thought. We are not separate from God, and we do not need to maintain a sense of worth outside that union. When we are trapped in the idea that we are independent individuals, we are also ensnared by a need to prove our value or overcome our flaws.

A skiing adventure I had serves to illustrate how ignorant and self-centered the ego-based mind can be. Many years ago, I was skiing a black (difficult) run that merged with a green (easy) run at the bottom. A skier ahead of me on the green run was moving slowly and appeared to be new to the sport. Since I felt good about my ability to do blacks, my mind began to speak.

Impatient and striving to go faster, I thought, *I'm such a better skier than—*. But before my mind could even finish the thought, I had skied through the orange barrier and down the side of the mountain out of bounds. I had been watching where I was going to avoid hitting the "slow" man ahead of me. Nevertheless, I went over the edge. I literally had no physical feeling or mental recollection of going over the cliff. It was almost as though I were lifted up and then just plunked down. I was skiing one second and at the bottom of a cliff the next.

When I landed facedown, my skis were off my boots and stuck on the side of the embankment with my poles. I was not hurt, but I was seriously humbled. *Okay, God, I hear you,* I thought. *I get that you can wipe me out before I even finish my self-centered thoughts. I hear you. There is no need for ego or judgment.* My mind had been on a roll about my superior skills, but obviously, that was not the view God had of the situation.

I stood at the bottom of the cliff and yelled up, "I'm okay! It's all right. I'm okay!" But apparently, no one had even noticed me as I went through the rope. I wasn't the center of anyone's world but my own.

After climbing up for my equipment, I slid back down and carried everything through the trees into open space. As I put my skis back on, I realized that when I had been wiped out, my ego had been slapped in the face. The incident gave me total clarity about how the mind can take a thought and run with it, causing damage by its arrogance and need to assert dominance.

As we move from a thought-based perception of life to a spiritual one, we will reshape our views of the past and how we live in the present. When false or misguided messages are culled, we begin to free the ego from its lack of worth, its self-importance, and the judgments made of us and by us.

When we change our focus and live from our spirit rather than through the intellectual, logical, and egotistical mind, we are open to seeing life from love's view. Love begins to flow, and judgment begins to wane. As it says in the Bible, "Love is patient, love is kind. It does not envy, it does not boast, it is not proud." (NIV, 1 Cor 13:1)

Emotions are also linked to our thoughts and are often tied to our histories. In most cases, we have been programmed at an early age to think, feel, or react as we do. Sadly, I witnessed this firsthand in the interaction between a father and son.

As I was standing in line for the ski shuttle one afternoon, a man and his son walked up and stood behind me, just as a pickup truck turned the corner looking for parking. Staring at the truck, the father said loudly, "Look at that f____ idiot. He thinks he's driving a f____ eighteen-wheeler. People in this f____ town are f____ stupid and don't know how to drive."

In a short period of time, I watched the father send multiple messages to his son. The child was about eight years old, and as he experienced his father's words and actions, he may have been learning from, or about, his father. He could grow up to model the behavior or grow up to make certain he didn't. I wondered what other influences the child had in his life and whether there was something or someone to combat that harsh experience. Regardless, the son was receiving mental and emotional input that would impact his life.

This encounter was a perfect example of how beliefs are passed from generation to generation. As angry as I felt with the parent, I realized that he had simply distributed experiences from his own past, and he wasn't consciously aware of his behavior or attitude. He had become what his environment had taught him to be, and unless he gained the wisdom to look at himself, he would not know to change, nor would he ever recognize the impact he had on his child. Among the potential positive outcomes were its impact on the child's self-awareness as he matured and how he might use the pain of the experience for his growth.

The key to freedom from negativity is examining and detaching from the thoughts that are not right for us. Our thoughts are not us, yet they run in endless loops as we react to the events in our lives. Thoughts make us feel as if our ideas represent who we are: *I don't have time for this nonsense. I really don't like my boss, and he sure doesn't like me. I'm never going to lose that weight.* We fully fall for the word "I" and believe that thoughts like these are irreversibly true.

I found myself observing my mind one sunny afternoon during that transition point between conscious and unconscious thought when I was somewhere between being awake and dozing off for a nap. It was one of the most freeing experiences I've ever had. I recognized the silly and endless loops of the mind.

My mind sounded as if it were at least six feet from me. I heard it thinking, in a sense, and as it rambled, "my" mind seemed to be talking for talk's sake. I was in the room, in my body, but I was detached enough to observe my mind. I was separated from my mind, and it was not the important part of me that I had previously believed it to be. It wasn't even in me. It was "over there" somewhere simply spewing out stuff. Some of the thoughts made sense, and others were just disconnected words, put together in a meaningless sequence.

Watching my mind allowed me to understand two things. First, the mind has no original thoughts. If we are thinking a thought, someone else has thought it before us. All thoughts come from input, which then becomes more output. Thoughts are "out there" somewhere, and as they come to us, we take them in and turn them around as though we had created them. In that experience, I instinctively understood that we have the capacity to simply observe our thoughts, feelings, and ideas. We don't have to own them or act on them. Either we take control of our minds or they take control of us.

Second, and most important, I realized that I am not my mind and its thoughts. I immediately recognized that I was fully present in my body yet separate from my mind as I observed it work. My mind was no more the source of me than my foot. So where does the mind live? If we try to point to its source, where it comes from, we can't. In light of that, should the mind really be given status as the main part of who we are?

Meditation is a regular practice for many. When we succeed in this practice, we find a quiet calm that has always been there, though it is normally covered up by chatter. Just the simple act of sitting down and putting our feet flat on the floor is grounding. It creates a sense of connection to the earth. Letting our bodies relax on a chair brings peace. Envisioning a bright white light around our hearts and breathing into it centers us. A moment without thoughts is like a mini-vacation.

Sometimes I find it difficult to quiet my mind to meditate. As an alternative, I sit and watch my thoughts, much as I did on that afternoon. It can be like watching a movie with surprise scenarios and scripts. *Oh, look at that one about how I have nothing fun to do today. And why am I thinking about what my mother said to me when I was twenty-seven? I'm going to get the flu this year. Wait, why do I believe I'll get sick?* I see the activity and let it go. *My book is stupid. I should stop writing. Nope, not going to let that discourage me.*

And on it goes. Watching the mind is entertaining if we don't take our thoughts seriously. Thoughts do not need to be absorbed into our being. We can acknowledge them, be with them, and then let them pass. Thoughts are only as accurate as all the external sources that created them. The only perspective that contains all the relevant facts and information is the perspective of Divine Consciousness. A big part of our work on the spiritual journey is to evaluate how reliable our perceptions are and how well they are serving us.

The list of beliefs we absorb or create is endless: Never be late. Always put others first. Men are more important than women. Rich people are selfish. I don't matter. It's best to live in the city. It's best to live in the country. Without a degree, I'm worthless. Reading is vital. Don't listen to your emotions. Beauty is very important. Using logic is the way to succeed. Resolving life's inequities is our duty. We must be saved. Being spiritual is flakey. Money makes me important.

All these ideas are just thoughts, not truths. Some we grab and hold on to. Others we let pass. But by examining our thoughts and personal or cultural beliefs, opinions, theories, and even dogmas, we can release them. This is how we begin to move out of a false sense of self-identity formed by what we hold on to. When we stop attaching to our thoughts, we begin to lose our self-created identity and enjoy our true identity as a beautiful unique expression of God.

We can be trapped by our ego-based thinking, as I was in my ski story, striving to feel good about ourselves. We can also be trapped in painful concepts about ourselves based on what has happened in our lives, as I was in the coal cellar experience. The mind will always be drawn into the drama of self, good or bad, past or present.

Letting go of thoughts frees us to live from our hearts. But we can't do that until we know where we are stuck. Because of the many painful ways in which I was abused so early in my life, I had to find the courage to see all that had happened. Then I had to open my heart to heal instead of keeping it closed as a means of protection. That has been difficult to do. When you are physically, mentally, emotionally, and sexually abused at a very young age, all you want is a wall of protection.

But we are not our thoughts, nor are we our experiences. Thoughts form about things that happen (our experiences), and yet, the things that happen to us do not define who we are. They happen *to* us; they are not us. It is vital to clean ourselves out. We can and will be the same beautiful creation of God that we were, originally, at the moment of our birth. It's called being born again. "I tell you the truth, unless you are born again, you cannot see the Kingdom of God." (NIV, John 3:3)

Unless we let go of all we believe ourselves to be, we will not be able to see who we really are as vessels of God. We have the capacity for a whole new life if we release ourselves and open up to a new reality.

Practice

Write down some of the norms and values you have absorbed. It's really pretty easy. For example, did your mom wear the pants or your dad rule the house? Did you have a really great teacher who encouraged you or a mean one? Did you grow up rich or poor? Any of these kinds of situations create beliefs. What beliefs were created in each case?

Write one negative and one positive belief you got from family, education, and the surrounding culture. Then, for each one, ask some questions: Is it true? Is it an absolute? Is it something I wish to continue believing?

Next, consider whether there is a thought that is dominant right now in the present. Is the thought related to a situation or person? What is it saying? Just think about what that thought is. Now ask whether it is true or partially true and how it makes you feel. Is the thought helping you? If not, can you let it go?

CHAPTER NINE

Releasing the Unintended

SUFFERING IS AN UNINTENDED CONSEQUENCE of being human. We aren't created to feel bad about anything or to have a negative experience of life. Generationally, we pass down ways of expressing love, sharing, and caring, and we pass down the flaws, limited perspectives, and biased attitudes. No parent or teacher sets out to impart negative views or to make a child feel bad. We are all products of where we came from, both in terms of our families and our cultures. We can choose to stay trapped in the beliefs we've inherited or created, or we can free ourselves.

Unfortunately, we can't pass down the liberating experience of waking up because it is an individual journey. We can, however, share our spiritual journeys, as I did with my children who believe strongly in intuitive knowing and use it regularly.

Waking up calls for self-examination, which can be hard. Most of us would just prefer to live our lives and not examine actions and thoughts. If we don't think it's broken, we don't want to fix it. If it feels good, we want to keep doing it. Regrettably, what pushes us to self-examination is usually pain, tragedy, loss, or anything else that makes life hard to handle. The dynamic of opposites pushes us toward something good (growth) by means of something bad (problems). The path of least resistance makes us stagnate.

Along my journey, I came to see that every time I turned to Spirit for guidance, I grew, especially in uncomfortable situations. When I didn't seek understanding, I'd go through another similar and difficult experience. If I didn't get the message that a certain behavior or belief was not good for me, I would experience the message in another form, giving me a second chance to learn, grow, and make progress as a person and on my spiritual journey. The bottom line of each lesson from God would be this: *It's my life, Mary, not yours. Let's heal you and get you out of the way. Your beliefs create the pain, but I can deal with it.*

What do we do with all the painful experiences we have in life? If we're normal, we try to fix them, get past them, or diminish them. Yet they are gifts. We argue and say, "No, God doesn't give us pain. That's not love. That's not grace." We don't want to believe that God corrects our course for us when we are on the wrong path. But even a self-aware adult will reach out to help a child by creating discomfort, such as calling for a time-out or a ban on electronics. The parent may ground the child or cancel an event. A serious conversation can also be a corrective measure. And in case you were wondering, God loves serious conversations.

Love often comes via the most painful circumstances. The hidden gift helps us wake up. Unfortunately, pain is also most often the only thing that gets our ego's attention. Whether it is financial loss, death, divorce, betrayal, or illness, such gifts serve to crack open our shells. God wants us to wake up to the beauty of our essential being, which is God existing as us. He wants to flow easily through our lives rather than bumping into pieces of our ego, left and right. The spiritual path is a journey of letting go, but we don't divorce our egos voluntarily, so we are assisted in releasing our blocks. And more often than not, the assistance comes in the form of discomfort. The pain of surgery is required to enable healing something that is broken.

I have benefited from the hard times as part of my awakening journey. It finally became obvious that if I didn't ask for wisdom from a problem, rather than fighting it, I would need to go around that mountain again. I even began to embrace the problems, admitting to God that I'd hit another brick wall and asking what I should see. One time the brick wall came as a double blow to help me end two unhealthy relationships. In the process, I released the idea that I needed anything or anyone, even relationships or friendships, to give me worth or a normal life.

This gift of pain came when I unknowingly dated a man who, for over a year, cheated and lied. (Yes, I wonder how I could have been so stupid or blind. We see what we want to see until we want to see the truth.) When the reality of his cheating hit me in my face one morning, I was completely devastated and couldn't muster the desire to fly out the next day for a planned girlfriend trip. I shared what happened with one of my travel companions, and she reacted to my pain by saying, "Get over it."

Now doubly hurt, I experienced my friend's reaction as the straw that broke the camel's back. I became very angry. This particular friend had behaved harshly toward me several times, even to the point of cruelty. At one point, I shared a painful memory of childhood sexual abuse. "Oh, *my* grandfather abused me. Get over it," she replied. (I later learned that she had not been abused by her grandfather. It had been a lie.)

The whole brick wall mess concerning my boyfriend and my friend's harsh reaction turned out to be a gift. These losses could have shattered me—and admittedly they did for a while—but because I was learning to look for the reason behind painful events, I was soon able to appreciate the gift. I needed to get angry. It wasn't healthy to have people in my life who lied and showed neither compassion nor support in my time of need. Letting them both go was an act of compassion toward myself, a healing experience, a gift of pain from which I could grow.

As an added gift, I let go of more ego. My life hadn't been lining up as I wanted, but I was open enough to see that my life didn't belong to me. Like Job, who lost everything, I gained the reward of better friendships down the road and a deeper understanding of love.

When those hard times come, we can make a choice. If we don't continue to learn and grow by making the choice to examine our lives, our choices will be tainted by experience instead of illuminated by truth. And our lives will continue to cycle between the opposites of good and bad. In the absence of self-reflection, experiences become more challenging in order to get our attention.

Every one of us can look back and ask ourselves what we were thinking. The answer is simple. At the time we make a choice, good or bad, our thoughts and emotions line up to move in a specific direction. We can only make the choices we are capable of making at any given time. In other words, if we knew better, we would do better. If we could, we would. We cannot be other than who we are in the moment—and neither can anyone else. Two minutes earlier, our choices might have been different. Two years later, our choices will be different.

We are where we are, and we cannot be somewhere else until we get there. How do we get to a healthier place? We make the choice to examine our perceptions, attitudes, our treatment of ourselves, and our relationships with others. We then alter what needs to shift.

According to psychiatrist Erik Erikson's eight stages of development, by the time a child is about twelve, his interaction with life has established his social and emotional development, including his sense of self, view of life, and comfort zone in the world. Consider some scenarios about which people have formed beliefs and how the beliefs formed from the same scenario might be translated in more than one way.

Let's say that two people have each had the experience growing up of their extended families getting together for a meal once a year to celebrate a particular holiday. One of these people may have concluded from their childhood experience that gathering as an extended family is a joyful event that keeps families connected in a positive way. But the other person may have concluded that getting together is what "good" families do, even if doing so is filled with stress and drama.

Here's another scenario—one in which a set of circumstances might be translated by a person in more than one way. If your family was always late when you were a child, you may conclude that being on time doesn't matter or that the agenda of others is not important. Conversely, you may feel embarrassed or translate it as rude and decide never to be late as an adult.

Another example of belief formation relates to ideas about work and accomplishments. If someone works hard to get good grades, yet no one acknowledges the accomplishment, the person may come to believe that hard work or accomplishment is of little importance in life, or worse, that she herself doesn't matter.

What do we do about the deeply held beliefs that we can't even see? Although they are not easy to detect, these beliefs can alter our behavior and our views about life. They form our self-perceptions, and because we don't realize they are there, we are powerless to change them. We become prisoners to the hundreds and thousands of subliminal "life-ads" about what is good or bad, right or wrong. And of course, we are also products of our life experience.

The bottom line is that an important determiner in how we experience the world is our conditioning, and that conditioning is impacted by our experiences, by the values and beliefs our families held that were adopted by us subconsciously, and by our unique, individual makeup.

Our paradigms are as limited as fish in a bowl. All the fish know is water. All we know is what we have learned growing up. This is why many women stay in abusive relationships, why boys follow in their father's footsteps, and why tradition is so engrained. As Irish statesman and philosopher Edmund Burke remarked, "Custom reconciles us to everything."

Choosing to examine life is automatically synonymous with change. It is the resolution to keep gaining wisdom, not just sticking with a particular perspective. It is the best way we have to correct misunderstandings, get new insights, change unproductive patterns, expand the quality and meaning of our lives, and awaken to who we are.

How can you do that? First and foremost, ask your inner Self what you need to do about your life. God wants healing and wholeness. His wholeness is in us, but when we believe we are separate, we lose that fundamental wholeness.

We can also ask questions of ourselves. When you get angry, ask why. Don't assume it is about the current situation. Dig deeper. When you are hurt by someone, soak in the feeling. Is it familiar? Can you label the feeling? Is it loneliness? Abandonment? Fear? Shame? These kinds of inquiries into our thoughts and feelings help us find their sources and release them.

Our willingness to see clearly is greatly improved when we choose to get out of our minds and be present with our hearts. We won't find a different view as long as we are tethered to the opinions created in our minds. Greater wisdom arises from the infinite spiritual realm, the realm created by Divine Consciousness. Change happens when we are on a path to awakening from illusion into reality.

It takes a long time to become the adults we are. Changing who we are will take time too. Reliving the disturbing memory of being confined to a coal cellar helped me understand why, as an adult, I expected to be treated as if I didn't matter and had no feelings. At four, I could not decipher my own inherent innocence or the truth that I was neither guilty nor bad. Nor could I understand that my mother had misplaced blame. Without the maturity to work through the situation, I interpreted her anger as proof that I was not meant to exist and should never have been born. I took my impressions as a four-year-old child and carried them into my identity as an adult.

Most of us are so stuck in illusions that we have no idea that the misconceptions exist. This is why it is vital to look at our lives and then go even deeper into the essence from which we came. We must embrace pain and discomfort in our current lives as well. Everything works together to wake us up and bring us to the fullness of ourselves. In the very end, if we are willing to open enough, we will have the capacity to embrace our true identities as spiritual beings.

Although suffering is an unintended consequence of human life, it can be used for the good. We can release things that don't fit who we are in our current lives. We can dig for the influences of which we are not consciously aware. Through the willingness to look at ourselves, our beliefs, and behaviors, we release more of the ego material that forms our self-identity, and we clear the channels for the Light to shine through.

We need to feel good about ourselves in order to let ourselves go. Everything about our view of life will change when we heal and let go. We will not need to protect, defend, or build ourselves up. We will let life flow because we'll be able to make the choice to say, "This is Your life God, not mine. You can have my free will."

Practice

Choose a problematic life situation about which you hold some emotions. Sit back, try to disengage, and just look at the situation. Close your eyes and try to take a detached view of yourself, the people, and the circumstances involved in this situation. Know that emotions are always attached to perceptions about experiences. How old do you feel? What do you really feel about the situation? How do you feel inside about the situation? What truths arise during your self-exploration?

Think about one belief you may have about yourself: *I'm not worthy. I'm not smart enough. I'm not athletic. My interest in the paranormal makes me weird.* Sit with whatever you came up with and think about where the belief came from. How did you come to believe that? Then ask yourself these questions: *Is this the truth? Why do I hang on to it? Did God create me to feel this way about myself?*

CHAPTER TEN

Living from the Inside Out

WHAT WAS THE FIRST CHOICE YOU MADE TODAY? Was it when to get up? What to wear? How you were going to interact with someone or respond to a problem? Did you think about what your attitude would be for the day, or did you just put on a familiar attitude like you put on your shoes?

How many thoughts have you had today so far? A thousand? Ten thousand? How many decisions have you made? Think about it. The endless stream of thoughts is exhausting.

Each day presents us with opportunities to see life from a deeper perspective. We can get up, do our morning routine, let our minds roll, and never ask what or why. Or we can get up and ask why we are doing what we do. We can wonder what motivates us to make a particular decision. We can rein our thoughts in. We can seek guidance for even the simplest of things. Or we can stop thinking altogether. If we stop thinking, we will continue to do things, but the action will feel spontaneous.

Some of the life choices we can make to begin our journey to awakening are captured in the following resolutions:

- I need to change.
- I seek wisdom more than knowledge.
- I practice listening to my heart, not my mind.
- I do not fear change, big or small.
- I am willing to give Spirit control of my life.
- I am willing to let my idea of a separate self die.

Life has so much to offer when we live from Spirit and can be much more peaceful when we choose to let the creativity of God flow through all we do without interruption. Within the confines of the five senses, we can't create room for what else could motivate us. Immersed in thinking, we fail to give credence to a deeper source of wisdom. We might say to our sense of self, as one might say to a self-centered teenager, "It's not all about you."

The first step to being open is to desire openness and be willing to drop everything we ever thought we knew about the universe, God, or ourselves. Yearn to start fresh. Hunger to be, not do.

How can we just be? We breathe and don't work to make it happen. We just breathe. We eat when we're hungry. We do not conjure up the idea of hunger. We feel it and automatically seek food. If we can grasp the idea of God living in us, as us, and instead of us, we don't need to figure anything out. We can never know the joy of living in the flow as long as we act and think as if we are in control. If we stop thinking and let go of ourselves, our lives and activities will continue, but they will just spring from another source.

Life takes care of itself. If we stop thinking and doing, life will not fall apart. It will grow in mysterious ways. Life will be more peaceful when we stop resisting it, and we will give and receive more love—automatically. It just happens. What stops the flow of life? Refusing to let go stops the flow of life. So does thinking we are in control, need to be in control, or even *can* be in control.

We fear not getting what "we" want if we let God take the lead. I've been there. I've thought that I would be helpless and not get the things I want if I let God take the lead. I've thought God might make me work at a job I didn't want. I've even thought that God might make me give up skiing! Fear is what makes us refuse to turn over the reins or even be unable to do so. When there is no you, there is no fear. Life just is what is.

Too many of us wait until life throws a curve and we are desperate for an answer before we seek spiritual guidance. Only when we can't fix our own problems do we turn to God. Why not turn your life over to God before the issues get so hard? Why not be open to anything and everything? Why not just let go and start enjoying your higher truth right now?

"But what if the wrong thing happens?" you ask in response. If you're already stressed, it already has. "But what if I believe the wrong thing?" But what if you *already* believe the wrong thing?

People who are rigidly adamant that they know the entire truth of God (or anything else, for that matter) stay miniaturized amongst the giant sequoias of their own beliefs. Those who are unwilling to change barricade themselves against a bigger reality, which is that God is bigger than any belief we may have.

The concept of letting go, or doing nothing, goes against all we have learned. "What do you mean I don't have to do anything? I have to get up. I have to look for a job, tell people I need one, and set up interviews," you might say. What I am saying is no, you don't. God is living in your body as you. Stop trying to take over.

After I had my experience of being consumed by the Light, I was completely enamored of God. Like meeting a superstar in the grocery store, my experience was striking—not something that happened and was quickly forgotten. The impact hung on. I did not know these experiences of God would happen to me, nor were they something I could have conjured up. It was a pure gift, and I was blown away that the light and peace of God would fill my room and me. I wanted more, so I simply asked for it.

I didn't desire another dramatic event. I just wanted God to be in control of my life. I had, after all, lost my job, and I needed to find one. So in total faith, as opposed to as a threat or challenge, I said, "If you can save me from the desire to die, you can surely find me a job." For one month, I sat and did nothing: no phone calls, no inquiries, and no asking people for suggestions or connections. I simply sat. Then one day I received a call from a friend telling me he'd just received his Chamber of Commerce newsletter. He suggested I call them for a job. I was a writer with a background in promoting companies, so it was not a completely unreasonable suggestion.

"Well of course I can't call them," I replied. "They obviously have someone doing their publications." My mind was using logic and throwing thoughts at me. But as soon as we hung up, my hand involuntarily picked up the phone book and dialed the Chamber. It was spontaneous action without thought—God in me, as me, making that phone call. I was invited for an interview the next day and offered the job the day after that. The person doing the newsletter was ready to retire and only staying until they found a replacement.

I didn't know about anyone wanting to retire, but God did. Had I taken the responsibility of finding a job myself, I might have accepted one that wasn't as well suited for me. But the job sent to me by God was just down the street from my children's school, my work hours were in harmony with my children's schedules, and I very much enjoyed the work.

Contrary to how it may seem, I was not being passive. I was actively trusting that God would find me a job. To actively trust is to engage the heart in knowing that the answer is coming. It is believing beyond what the human mind can know. "Now faith is confidence in what we hope for and assurance about what we do not see." (NIV, Heb 11:1)

I believed in the invisible with all my heart. Not everyone receives the presence of God's light in their room, by which to affirm the existence of another source beyond the human plane. But everyone can seek God with passion and let him control their lives. Everyone can be open to this divine source as truth.

We do not need to make life happen. God never asked for help to create life and life never asked us to sustain it. Life happens on its own. We see it everywhere. It seems we human beings are the only creations on planet Earth that believe we need to be in control. But without the end of the ego and until we wake up, we can't and won't let go of trying to make things happen. We must ask ourselves at which point in our lives we decided that we were smarter than the creator of life itself?

We have no way of knowing what will happen if we make the choice to let Source be in control. Source will sustain its creations, and because it manifests as us in individual form, it is safe to let Source flow to us and through us without knowing where we are going or what will happen. What we need to do is surrender the outcome and give in to the process. Just as I did not have the foresight to conceive of an editor who would be retiring, no one else can see ahead to what may be out there as a plan for their life.

In reality, no one knows what will happen in the next two minutes or two days. We simply imagine we are in control, which is what gives us the illusion of comfort. We may *think* we're going to get groceries on Friday, have friends over to dinner on Saturday, watch a movie with the kids on Sunday, and go to an important meeting with a client on Monday. And then a tornado hits on Thursday. We survive, but everything we own is gone. What happens to our plans then? And what happens to the sense of power we had when we thought we were in control? It was illusory, but it often takes some major event like a tornado to inform us of that.

But what happens if we have deep faith and give God permission to be in control? What happens if we surrender control? What if we actively trusted God rather than ourselves? What if we actively became passive? What if we chose to be the passenger and not the driver? Does that sound too radical?

Who would do that? Someone who doesn't believe they have all the answers. Someone who can't make life work. Someone who can get past the ego. Someone who understands that we are far more than the individual life-dramas in which we find ourselves.

When I was raising my children, we struggled financially too many times. In one very difficult period, I opened the kitchen cabinet, looking for dinner, and there was only the box of cereal we'd had for breakfast. In utter despair and frustration, I pounded my fist on the counter and cried, "I want to take my kids out for pizza." I wasn't telling anyone. I was having a serious vent.

But from behind me, I heard authoritative words, "Take them to the Upper Crust," which was an upscale restaurant in suburban Atlanta. I looked around and saw that no one was there, but I heard the voice a second time. "Take them to the Upper Crust."

I knew God was giving me an answer, and I had a choice to make. I could either ignore what I heard or trust that God was bigger than my problem. I had no money, no credit cards, and no way to buy dinner, but I walked into the den and said, "Hey kids, let's go out for pizza."

What was I thinking? What was I doing to my children? Would I end up in jail? What would make me jump off this cliff of faith? The answer was clear. I either believed that God was in control or not. I could live with one foot in and one foot out of the arena of faith or I could plant both feet in him. That night I made the choice.

As we stood in line waiting to be seated, I felt terrified. Soon we were shown to our table, the waiter appeared and we ordered. Trying to make myself calm, I put my hands in my lap and focused on my children's conversations. After a while, I glanced to the side and saw the couple that had been ahead of us in line. They had finished their meal and were leaving. It had been well over an hour since we'd ordered. I wondered if the waiter knew we couldn't pay and had called the police, but I sat quietly with no intention of asking for a thing.

Suddenly our waiter rushed up saying, "I am so sorry you haven't received your meal. I'll have it out in five minutes." When he brought the pizza, he put it on the table and ceremoniously sliced open the deep-dish pie. In unison, my three children groaned. It was all vegetables, not what my young kids had ordered. Frustrated and embarrassed, the waiter assured us that the correct pizza would be out quickly.

"Thank you, it's *really* okay," I assured him as he rushed back to the kitchen.

Before I could panic again at what I was doing, I noticed a man walking towards our table. "Good evening," he said. "I'm the manager. I understand that you waited over an hour for your meal and when it arrived, it was the wrong pizza."

I smiled and just nodded, desiring to be almost invisible.

He apologized and said, "Your entire meal is on us."

That was it. God spoke to me, and I listened. I took a giant leap of faith, which made no sense to my mind. But I wasn't listening to my mind. I was listening to my heart. My heart was willing to jump off a cliff to have the deepest relationship with God I could. I was willing to let go of my human reality and let Divine Consciousness be in control.

Moving forward on our spiritual paths involves making the choice to open our hearts to change. There is more life than we can ever imagine when we stop living from the limits of our minds and freely open to the flow of God in our hearts. We don't need to figure everything out—or really *anything*. Life will just happen. Life is guaranteed to happen. The breath of God will not stop, and when it moves, it moves through each of us.

Each of us can have a Red Sea moment in which God parts the waters so his chosen people may escape the valley of hardship. We are all God's chosen children, but we don't always know that we are. I obeyed the voice I heard and took my children for pizza without any money.

When we live by faith, God will act on our behalf. The calling of your heart will move you forward when you break the shell of your mind. And once you feel and trust that "other knowing" and are willing to live from the inside out, there is no going back. All the fullness of life awaits us when we are willing to embrace it.

Practice

One way to develop trust is to precede our efforts with a request. "If I am meant to do this, open the door. If not, close it." Just make a simple, honest statement about allowing God to open or shut the door to whatever it is you want to do or have. Start with baby steps.

What is it that you need in your life? A job? A partner? A vacation? Do what you can to make it happen, but ask to be stopped if it's not right. Be willing to let another answer show up.

Another way to obtain guidance is to act on what you think or feel you are being guided to do and see what happens. When you feel a gut instinct about what to do, take a step and use the experience in a process of trial and error. The action can be about something small or it can be huge, but do whatever is outside your comfort zone. Do it as though you were jumping off a cliff and expecting to be caught. The bigger the leap, the bigger the surprise.

Sit quietly and listen for your guidance.

CHAPTER ELEVEN

Spiritual Paths

ALL OF US ARE UNIQUE INDIVIDUALS who take many different paths to Spirit. But because we have been exposed to spiritual practices such as yoga and meditation, more and more Westerners carry out their search beyond the basics of a doctrine. Our culture is becoming increasingly comfortable with personal spiritual experiences rather than organized formats that require a personal self who can believe and follow guidelines. Seeking outside of such confines allows our spiritual path to emerge from the core of who we are as manifested beings.

Spirituality can be a process, practice, system, or ability. Trying to define spirituality can be like trying to define color. For example, if someone has never seen yellow, what can you say about it? It's lighter than orange but brighter than tan. It's not as deep as gold but warmer than cream. The definition depends on what you know of color, what you can begin to imagine, and how much you are willing to explore. If we stop our exploration of spirituality or put limits on it, we don't get the whole picture.

Many years ago, I attended a class titled "A Course on Mysticism" that was led by Rev. Lawrence Palmer, who was first a Baptist and then a Unity minister. In his course, he described three approaches to spirituality: that of traditional religion (any kind), metaphysics, and mysticism. The goal of all three is for us to grow, but it's interesting that the one least often chosen of the three is the most direct. The least chosen is also the only one that calls for the sacrifice of the ego. It is mysticism.

Traditional religion is founded, principally, on humanity's imperfections and the need for God. The desire or need to find God automatically creates the concept of separation: I'm here. He's there. Separation then begets worship, which develops into a system by which we do things to gain the favor of or to please God. Our practices and beliefs are turned into rules and guidelines to help us be in right relationship with our personal belief about God.

The natural result of traditional religion is struggle because of its implicit belief in separation and sin-consciousness. The goal is to reform or fix oneself. Traditional religion can be a starting place, but we must become aware that it is not necessarily the finish line. When we realize we are not separate from God and that the kingdom of heaven is within us, sin-consciousness and the need to be fixed fall away.

Metaphysics depends on universal principles, which can create specific outcomes on the Earth plane. Because Spirit is energy, metaphysics uses the laws of cause and effect. Our energy (thoughts, behaviors, and actions) create specific effects that manifest our lives as we know them. Metaphysics makes use of spiritual laws to reach a result, though a connection with God is not absolutely necessary.

In metaphysical practice, it is necessary to actively "work the law" through practices like visualization or affirmation. The focus of this type of practice is to gain specific outcomes such as health, wealth, or personal change. The goal in metaphysics is to make things happen through the power of universal energy. By implication, metaphysics gains outcomes via an active system of the will rather than through the dissolution of the will.

Metaphysics can get us more success and can do that without causing us to connect with pure Divine Consciousness. The downside is that metaphysics may trap us within the struggle of a self that keeps trying to use divine power. Through metaphysics, we keep our self-identity and ultimately, our problems. We continue to live in duality—even if we obtain success in manifesting along the way.

The third spiritual path is mysticism, entailing the loss of self. Mysticism means allowing oneself to let go of a personal identity. Mystics have insight into mysteries transcending ordinary human knowledge. They often live from a direct communication with the divine, and they experience immediate intuition. The ego disappears and Divine Consciousness flows through the human expression.

Eastern religions are primarily based on the ideal of no-self. However, contemplative Christians, who have eperienced nondual consciousness, have also been mystics in union with God. Figures like Thomas Merton, Thomas A Kempis, Meister Eckhart, and Mother Theresa were mystical Christians.

In the United States, the journey towards mysticism is growing as we expand our spiritual seeking beyond the confines of doctrine and limiting assumptions about separation between the human and the divine. According to some surveys, our churches are in decline because people are seeking something more than the laws of religion and long to have a spiritual experience that will change their lives.

Mysticism is unfathomable for the reason that it cannot be known to someone who has not experienced it. It is touching a reality not known in our normal human existence. In 2002, I touched that mysterious realm in a near-death experience (NDE).

On October 22, 2002, I was driving to Denver for some shopping. It had been snowing and cloudy from where I lived in the mountains until I came out of the Eisenhower Tunnel on Interstate 70. It had stopped snowing, but the skies were still gray. I could not see the black ice on the road ahead, and as my wheels hit it, the car began spinning in circles. Seconds later, it veered toward the median and flew nose-over-tail three times before landing on the interstate, going in the opposite direction.

On the middle flip, time slowed, and I realized I was hanging upside down, trapped by my seatbelt. My head was pressed to the driver-side window and my hands were gripped so tightly on the steering wheel that it was bent. I looked to my right and the passenger dashboard began to glow yellow.

In one instant there was yellow, and then I was gone. There was no car, no steering wheel, no dashboard—and no me. I was once again in pure white light, as I had been so many years before during the experience in my bedroom. Only this time, I was without a body.

I had no identity as Mary and no physicality by which I was confined. Gazing into the white light, I was in a pure state of being. I did not *have* peace, nor was I *at* peace. As pure being, I *was* peace. The white light, total awareness, and peace were pervasive. I was in it, yet as it. I was pure being, and I was all that existed in those moments in infinity. There were no thoughts, only complete awareness of existing fully without form. In the light, I, as the essence of being, was complete: whole, calm, aware. I was the infinite and eternal. Time was not a factor. There was no space or time. There was only infinite existence and pure peace. What must have been seconds felt like the endlessness of forever.

Suddenly, from somewhere that felt outside of pure being, came a thought. *Will I live or will I die?* It was just a thought, and the two potential outcomes were equal. It absolutely didn't matter. And though it didn't matter, a response echoed, *I don't want to die.* I didn't have a sense of it being me, so I can only conclude that Divine Being knew it wasn't my time to die.

As soon as that response came, I was immediately back in my body in the car, experiencing the last flip as it crashed onto the ground. Not a single window was intact, and shards of glass covered my body. Every inch of the car had either been dented or crushed. In shock, disoriented, and still gripping the steering wheel, I looked through an empty front window and whispered, "Somebody help me. Somebody please, help me."

Seemingly out of nowhere, a man walked up to the car with my cell phone and asked, "Did you lose this? Let me call 911."

I suffered little physical damage, only cuts on my legs, neck, and forearms and a concussion. In shock for several days, I felt completely foreign in human surroundings. The experience was traumatic for me, not for the terrible accident, but for the total loss of my human self into the form of pure Being. I had experienced myself as the Consciousness of God, and it took more than two years before I could speak of it without crying "I want to go home."

My life on Earth in a physical body was unexpectedly draining. It was deeply challenging, both mentally and emotionally, and living was like wading through water up to my chest. Being human was tedious, slow, and exhausting. Everything felt heavy, and I felt lost. I wanted the freedom of just being without the restrictions of a body, mind, or reactive feelings. I wanted to go back to who I was as pure Spirit.

Many years later, I realized that the only way to feel I was home again was to live from Spirit by the willingness to let my ego-identity go. It would be another seven years before I would experience home and the letting go of self for a third and final time.

My NDE gave me a taste of union with God. Mysticism is about such union. The oneness happens through the surrender of self-identity. It is the path to no-self. A mystical journey is one in which a person is chosen by God through surrender. By contrast, traditional religion puts the onus on *us* to choose *him*.

My first adult encounter with God as pure light and peace in my bedroom came from my deep, unconditional cry of surrender, which was not a surrender in the mind but a cry from the core of my being. My next encounter with the Light was during my NDE with complete surrender to everything, including even the loss of my physical form.

The outcome of mysticism is selflessness, which is the sacrifice of the self. It is crucifixion. The sacrifice involves not the body, but the belief in a "me" as separate from God. The goal of the mystical journey is oneness with God.

I have never consciously pursued a metaphysical journey, but I did have an experience in which both the metaphysical and mystical were at play when God told me to give my car to a young woman in need. Naturally, I replied that I, too, needed a car and asked what I was going to do without one. As usual, I didn't get an answer. I just got direction. By this point on my journey, I had learned to yield to guidance because I had come to trust God more than I trusted myself. I gave my car away.

The next thing I knew, God was directing me to lay hands on a car at a nearby dealership. I was guided to walk into an automobile showroom and, in front of God and everyone else, put hands on a car and pray for it to be mine! *Seriously God? This is not me. You know my roots are in a very conservative Midwest suburb and in a Scandinavian family to boot. We don't do drama!*

At first, the act of laying hands on a car and bowing my head to pray felt humiliating and embarrassing. But rather than react, I continued to trust and just did as I was guided. This car incident was not done out of any religious belief about the laying on of hands. Such practices were not part of my journey. To act in a manner to manifest an outcome reflected metaphysical principles, and for me, mysticism rather than metaphysics was the basis of my journey. I simply had the pure desire to do whatever I had been guided to do, and the heck with my ego or my thoughts about it.

Each day for two weeks, one friend or another (great, adventurous people) drove me to the Honda dealership closest to my home. Feeling very self-conscious, I walked in and quickly chose the car closest to the door. Each friend took a side, placed hands on the car, and bowed their heads.

No one prayed out loud or made a bigger show than the one we were already making. God did not tell me how to do it. Thankfully, he had not told me to get down on my knees, place a Bible on the car hood, lay my hands on the Bible, and pray out loud. Instead, we just quickly did our thing and left.

After seeing us each day for some time, the salesmen finally asked what was happening. I'd already gone that far, so I was just honest about it. "God told me to give my car away, so I did. Then he told me to come in here and pray for a new one." There was no lying about what we were doing. What would be the point of lying? Human humiliation? I was already uncomfortable, so what more did it matter? Nothing about this was normal.

Because my journey was filled with unusual experiences and guidance, I got to the point where I no longer argued with guidance because answers or some necessary proof always came from my willingness to follow Spirit. Answers addressed my human problems, while the proof showed me that trust was all it took. I was becoming a vessel, but it came at the price of losing my pride—and that was the point.

After my explanation, the salespeople verbalized a long drawn out "Ooohhh" and snickered. But after several visits, they appeared to admire our tenacity and became our squad of cheerleaders. In fact, we turned into such a phenomenon that the dealership wanted to keep track of me. We exchanged phone numbers.

When the car we had laid hands on was sold to someone else, the head of the sales department called to express his regret that the car was gone. He sounded very awkward in voicing his concern. After two weeks of making fools of ourselves by worldly standards, I asked myself, *Well, now what?*

Then I unexpectedly got a phone call from my ex-husband. "I think I'm supposed to give you my car," he said. I was shocked because I had not told him or asked him anything. He just called to say he was shown he needed to give me his new blue Honda. He kept his ten-year-old truck for himself.

Though the car episode was both a metaphysical and mystical experience, I was definitely on a mystical path. I was moving into nonduality by letting go of my mind's ways of figuring things out and surrendering my ego-self with it. As my journey continued, I lost more and more of myself, and eventually, the idea of a separate self would be gone.

A mystical journey is like living in a continual burst of truth. It frees us from our limited sense of life and places us in a more authentic reality. Despite the fact that mystical experience conflicts with the assumptions of the mind, it has definite validity. Miracles all conflict with logic: turning water into wine; feeding the multitude with five loaves and two fishes; raising someone from the dead.

As we embrace our identity as God, the outcome will be to live in a balanced and integrated way with body, mind, and spirit merged. The laws of the universe become ours because a piece of the universe is what we are. As spiritual beings, we live from Divine Consciousness through the mind and body, and not as the mind and body while looking to Spirit for help.

What do we gain by living from Spirit rather than from the mind and body? Everything, with peace coming first.

When we are out of the way and believe with our whole being that God is fulfilling our lives, we relax. We live from wisdom rather than knowledge and from acceptance rather than judgment. Our paths are directed towards our talents, interests, gifts, and capabilities. Doors open that are meant to be opened. They are not forced open by what we think should be. And we are no longer prisoners of perception, false beliefs, or what human nature thinks ought to be the case. The key to living by Spirit, not mind, is to look at the difference between knowing, which is the field of the mind, and understanding, which is in the realm of Spirit.

Knowing is conscious, provable, objective, and active (like the word *doing*). Knowing is about something "out there," which means that there is distance between us and the object or concept we know. Knowing is dual.

Understanding is subjective, deep, often not provable, and personal. What we understand has a quality of being part of us and is therefore nondual. Understanding is wisdom that comes from experience. Knowledge involves reading or analyzing how to do something; wisdom involves actually doing it. There are three ways that we can practice living from Spirit rather than mind. We can tame the mind, meditate, and develop our intuition. Ultimately, they all require surrender.

Practice

Look at your journey. Are your experiences religious, metaphysical, or mystical? Center yourself in your heart and ask yourself which type makes you comfortable. Then consider how you want to be and how you want to grow in the next phase.

CHAPTER TWELVE

Stopping the Mind

THE EGO, OUR SELF-IDENTITY, gives importance to being somebody. Again, it's because our Western culture has trained us to grow the ego and its perception about who it is. Conversely, the spiritual path leads us to being nobody, which in turn leads us *not* to becoming nothing but to becoming everything. The goal of the spiritual path is not to obtain anything or improve ourselves but to let go of who we think we are and what we have done.

It is difficult to let go of everything, but it is also very freeing. In letting go, we can give up the struggles we face in an accomplishment-oriented world. The shift is to let spiritual intelligence—which has no limitations, does not compare, and is not bound by anything—flow through us. Spirit has nothing to do with what we have accomplished or could accomplish in life, because Spirit doesn't have to do anything. Spirit simply is, and as consciousness, it is everything.

To tame the mind, we come to understand that we have been prisoners of our thoughts. They have defined everything we know, everything we are, and everything we believe. But we can escape our thought-based prisons by releasing our thoughts. As I said before, thoughts float by like clouds. They will always be there. We just don't have to grab them anymore.

The first step in not grabbing them is to realize that we don't have to figure anything out. We grab and hold onto a thought when we believe we have to make choices. Should I call them or not? Do I sign it or not? If I don't buy it now, will I even be able to later? When we lose ourselves to the source of life, we don't need to stress over what to do. There is a whole universe working for us, in us, and as us. All that we need or could want can be provided.

I used to think the following scripture meant that God was all around me and was always with me. "For in him we live and move and have our being." (NIV, Acts 17:28) But now I see that it literally means *in* him. Like fish in water, we are contained within God. Everything is in him because he is everything. We live, move, and have our being in, as, and of him. It's absolutely literal. We are therefore free to let Life guide and direct. After all, Life is bigger, wiser, and more powerful than what our minds can conjure, and its timing is perfect.

Two questions then arise: How can I live without the activity of the mind and thought? How can I know something without thinking about it? The answer to both of these questions is that once we take ourselves off the throne of designated decision maker, wisdom just flows. We don't block it anymore. It takes practice, experience, and trust to let go of ourselves. In essence, it means the death of ego to gain the life of God.

A certain verse in the Bible kept calling to me, especially after I left the church. "I have been crucified with Christ and I no longer live, but Christ lives in me." (NIV,

Gal 2:20) I wondered what Paul meant and finally realized I needed to die to self. Ownership needed to go, and it would only happen by the death of my ego. It was the only way for me to be one with God.

But as we might ponder the fate of ego, another question arises: How do we get out of the way? The only escape route is to surrender our concept of self and the thoughts that feed it. The key is to stop believing what we think. The mind is not who we are, but in our separate human experience of life, as long as we are up and active, the mind is going nonstop. The fact that the mind is always active does not mean that we need to pay attention to it. We don't.

Let me give you an example of how to conquer our thoughts. There was a time in my life when I suffered from depression. As I began to understand that the depression had nothing to do with my true self, I learned to speak to the depression and question its components. I learned that my depression was composed of a series of thoughts and beliefs about my life, which in turn were creating feelings. I realized that my mind, thoughts, and emotions weren't the only show in town. I was just watching the same movie, over and over. There were other movies to watch, but I was stuck in that one.

Once I gained this insight, I began to exercise my spiritual muscles and literally started to talk to my thoughts and feelings as though they were another person. I confronted them as though they were real—which I had obviously thought they were previously. I said, "Okay emotions, you can be in the pits. Body, you can drag around if you need to, and stomach, because you reflect my emotional pain, you can ache if you desire. Mind, you can be despondent if you choose to be, but I am going to the grocery store. Who are you to mess with me anyway?"

It felt as though I had made the decision to be separate from those negative things instead of *being* them. They were just thoughts and reactions to thoughts, and they did not define me.

Then I envisioned putting those thoughts and that negative energy into a small black box. Mentally, I put the box on the wall as though I were hanging a picture. I stood up, straightened my clothes, got my purse, and headed to the store. For me, it was a powerful experience to choose between the thoughts of my mind and my authentic Self. Afterall, God is not depressed.

Speaking to those thoughts as though they were another person allowed me to question them. The mind hates that. We take away its power when we say, "Who's talking to me? From where did that thought come? What is this thing called 'my mind?'" Here is a key point: The more we question the mind, the weaker it gets.

The thoughts of the mind can be pictured as dust balls. One dust ball is floating by, waving its arms to be noticed. But if we blow it off, figuratively or literally, and refuse to acknowledge it as real by grabbing at it, then it floats away from us. Trust me, another will come, but we can do the same thing with it. The more we don't grab, the more the thoughts will stop trying to get our attention. In essence, they begin to give up.

The more we confront the mind, the less we believe in it. It's like having a nightmare. You wake up terrified or in a panic. It feels so real. But the more you awaken, the more you tell yourself that it was just a dream and not real. Then your breathing calms, your heart slows down, and you begin to see clearly that it really was just a dream. As you do that, its impact on you grows weaker and weaker. Such is the mind. Challenge its validity and it begins to fade.

Though I had put the mind in its place by saying I wasn't buying it, I did not ignore or bury my suffering. When I was ready, I dug in and healed the cause of my depression. But prior to that, I used speaking to my thoughts as a tool that enabled me to grow spiritually in spite of my problems. Speaking to my thoughts helped me separate from them and connect to my authentic self, the Spirit of God. When the noise of thoughts is stilled, we can begin to hear the voice of God.

In knowing that we are spiritual beings expressed as humans, we realize that what happens is not personal, but earthly. Things are happening to us, in our roles, in this time and space. But more importantly, they are happening *for* us. The people and events in our lives are there for the purpose of helping us wake up to our true identity. Don't take anything personally. God created a playground—the world—and he is playing in it as us. He is experiencing himself in many forms and scenarios, and he loves it.

Meditation is another tool for taming the mind and forging a deeper connection with Spirit. It is also useful for stress reduction and improved health. Call it a mental power nap because we let go of the mind. Meditation quiets our perceptions, allowing for the possibility of falling into the infinite consciousness of God.

The word "meditation" derives from the Sanskrit word *medha*, which means "doing the wisdom." What a great term. It implies that we may actively connect to the divine Self by opening the heart and quieting the mind.

Meditation has been thoroughly studied by both the scientific and medical communities, and it has been found to have numerous benefits. Meditation reduces stress, increases well-being, builds connectedness, fosters empathy, improves focus and memory, helps with creativity, and diminishes physical and emotional pain.

This practice is about quieting the mind rather than leaving it behind. Meditation is an art form, and personally, I am anything but an artist. This is how meditation goes for me. I begin with an intention by settling myself comfortably on a chair. I close my eyes and focus on my breathing. All goes well for about twelve seconds. Then the first thought comes. *I need to call the plumber*, and off I go along a train of thought. *Who shall I call? They're all so expensive. But maybe the neighbor knows someone.* Then I have the sudden realization that I am thinking, and I regroup.

I settle in again, refocused, breathing slowly. All goes well, briefly. *I forgot to pick up the cleaning. This is the third time I have forgotten it. If I don't go soon, they'll give my clothes away.* After realizing I'm thinking again, I regroup . . . again.

The mind is like an unruly child who just doesn't want to behave—and with good reason because the mind thinks it's you. If it settles down or it is quiet, we won't pay any attention to it. We will realize we don't need it, and if we learn to bypass it, it can't run the show. Meditation is a threat to the mind's importance, and even to its existence. What I'm saying is that we are control freaks, and the mind is our weapon.

There are several basic forms of meditation. Transcendental meditation uses mantras to keep the mind from interrupting and to focus. The mantra doesn't matter. It can be any word or phrase of choice: one, peace, love, spirit—anything. *One. Oh no, the dogs are barking. One. I hear the radio. One. One. My knee hurts. One. One.* Keep bringing the mind back to the mantra. It doesn't even matter how successful or unsuccessful you are. The intention is the connection.

In breathing meditation, the focus is on the breath: in and out breathing. You can use music to distract yourself. I am not good at meditation, but when I practice it, I use Native American drumming and chanting music, which takes me into another realm. I lose myself in the beat.

Another form of meditation is called the question/answer meditation. It's for restless people, like me, who find it challenging to completely quiet the mind. Personally, I love this type of meditation and use it often. The method is to sit and ask Spirit questions such as, *What do I need to know?* or *What could make me feel gratitude in this moment?* This technique opens us to experiencing a higher way of feeling, knowing, and being.

By taming, discarding, or quieting the mind, we let go of the constant pull of the ego. We let go of negativity about ourselves and others. We let go of judgments, comparisons, and all the other ways humans so easily fall prey to the assessments of the mind. And we stop damaging ourselves.

As I was listening to an audio book on Audible one morning while washing windows, I grasped the meaning of a familiar scriptural verse. Although I had read the verse many times, I had never had such a great aha as I did while washing those windows. The narrator referenced Matthew. "In everything, do to others what you would have them do to you." (NIV, Matt 7:12)

I stopped, stood up, and said, "Oh my gosh. I get it." I realized that I am not separate from God and he is not separate from anyone else. Therefore, anything I say or do to another is what I am also saying or doing to myself. If I say or think something negative about another, I am saying or thinking something negative to myself. My words are simultaneously about another and toward myself, whether the words are attacking and criticizing or supportive and praising.

I was suddenly given another insight about another piece of scripture: "You shall love your neighbor as yourself." (NIV, Matthew 22:39) It's not just that I should love or treat my neighbor as I would like to be treated. I should love my neighbor as if he *were* me—because he *is* me! God is me. God is my neighbor. God is every person, everywhere.

In that aha window washing moment, I saw that everything I did or said impacted me, my life, and my sense of love and being loved. In that moment of enlightenment, I made a commitment to watch my thoughts and words, knowing that we reap what we sow.

Although our culture is focused on the idea of being somebody, the true fullness and peace of life is about being nobody. Being nobody is not a void. Rather, a nobody has the life of God in its fullness. To help us live in a nondual world, we need to stop grabbing at the thoughts of the mind. They are not our thoughts and they are not us. They are just fragments of or energy patterns in the universe. Yet they feel like they belong to us. Thoughts encourage the concept of self-identity and keep us separated from God.

When we pay attention to what we are thinking, we see how ensnared we are in the endless loop and trap of thoughts in the form of ideas, concepts, beliefs, opinions, plans, and theories. Most thoughts are negative, and we can actually emotionally spin out of control just by the impact of them. But if they can't snag us, thoughts begin to give up, or perhaps more correctly, we don't notice them as much. And therefore, they don't get our attention and are not able to control our lives.

We can quiet the mind through meditation. We can put our minds in time-out and open to the voice of Spirit, which comes from within. Ultimately, we can discard the chattering of the mind when we see it as a false identity and no longer entertain it. This is the end goal of being fully awake and living only from Source, or God. When we reject the mind, when we see it as a bothersome insect buzzing in the air somewhere, we are free of it and its impact on our lives and beliefs. We are no longer defined by it, and we don't let it make us worry or influence our actions. We then allow the One Life that is in us to flow freely.

Divine Consciousness is the feeling that comes from the heart, whereas thoughts don't feel centered in us. We can end our own suffering by watching what we grab at or produce as thought. In the end, we can learn to live without the weight of thought. That doesn't mean we don't engage with ideas, we just engage from the Source within that is all of life.

Practice

In addition to the mind-quieting methods already provided, another way to curb our thoughts is to write them down and look at them objectively.

Write down an issue you are dealing with, and under it, write down the thoughts you are having about this issue. They don't need to be in order or even to make sense. Just write them down. This allows you to look at them rather than owning them. It gives you the ability to see issues from a point of detached observation rather than being pulled into believing that they belong to you.

CHAPTER THIRTEEN

Developing Your Intuition

MANY WORLD-FAMOUS AND SUCCESSFUL PEOPLE—including Albert Einstein, Steve Jobs, author Dean Koontz, and award-winning actor Alan Alda—have spoken of intuition as a basis for living. In fact, intuition has proven so important to living a good life that authors like Sonia Choquette and Malcolm Gladwell have devoted a lot of text to the subject and its application to everything from everyday life to business success.

Dr. Jonas Salk, developer of the polio vaccine, likened intuition to gifts tossed up from the sea. He was right. They are free, they are a surprise, and you don't have to do anything to get them. Moreover, when the gift is an intuition, it's just for you.

Intuition can be our best friend. All-knowing intuition comes from Divine Consciousness, which is the very cells of our being. Intuition knows all the tomorrows, all the circumstances we can't see, and all the possibilities beyond human comprehension. Intuition is the voice of Spirit giving us guidance, direction, and comfort. It happens spontaneously, without our having to work at it. We know something, but we don't know why.

As the human world feels more and more unreliable, we are turning to alternatives in all areas of life.

In medicine, we're using acupuncture, herbs, chiropractic, and homeopathy. With the foods we eat, we are becoming more aware of what is causing poor health. We are choosing organic or gluten free foods and consuming fewer processed goods.

We are also turning to alternative ways of knowing. We don't as easily trust what we hear, what others believe, the way behavior is manifesting, or how standards are being redefined as we once did. We live in tension on a local, national, and global level. As the world becomes less dependable, we have the choice to receive information and guidance from a more reliable source: God, Universe, Infinite Essence of life.

People are not looking for peace and security from the outside, which isn't providing it, but from Source, which is within. To have a constant and direct connection with that guidance, we need to use our intuition.

Intuition is a sudden knowing or awareness that arises from the core of our beings. It simply feels right, truthful, and grounded. We cannot think it into being, analyze anything to attain it, create it, or make it happen. We simply just know something without any source for the knowledge other than the feeling of truth that lies within. But that feeling of truth is so deep it cannot be denied.

Moving through life without intuition is like vacationing in a car with a flat tire. The ride is very bumpy. But if we rely on intuition for guidance, it may feel to us like taking a risk because intuition often goes against our culture, education, and modern theories. We are taught to make it on our own through "sweat equity," while intuition comes spontaneously without our effort. Regardless of the fact that intuition is a gift, most people would say intuition doesn't make sense, it isn't logical, and it's actually silly. And if we buy into it, we are making it up.

On 9/11, I was in front of the bathroom mirror doing my hair when I got an overwhelming urge to turn on the television. I was living in the Midwest, and it was around 8:00 a.m. I had not spoken with anyone that morning and had no idea what was happening in the world. But I felt a very strong urge in my gut telling me to go to the den and turn on the television. It would not go away, so I listened to it. I walked down the hall and turned on the TV just as the plane hit the second tower.

Why in the world would I feel an urge to turn on the TV? Why would I even listen to such an urge? My mind certainly didn't think it made sense. But I listened because it was coming from somewhere that wasn't me, and it wasn't even logical. Those are two sure signs that Spirit prompted this urge. I needed to be aware of what was happening.

Intuition is something that just pops up as a flash of understanding, a sudden aha, or an impulse to do something. It can be a spark of insight or an unexpected feeling to pursue a hunch. It literally comes out of nowhere, having no reason or logic. We cannot conjure it up, no matter how hard we try. All we can do is ask Spirit to help us receive it.

Intuition is the most consistent way of living from Spirit, and while it takes practice to hone, it is not a practice but a way of being. Intuition is passive. It just comes. The mind uses analytical thinking and problem solving.

The constant attempt to solve things stands like a thick fog between our need to know and the answer. Intuition doesn't need problem solving. It simply knows.

We are taught to live in our heads, to embrace external input, and to figure things out. We are given courses in math, science, and even psychology—which are all about the mind. Our educational system does not offer courses in intuition because intuition is not logical. Sadly, we are actually taught to dismiss hunches and gut feelings.

To live by intuition means we must believe an invisible energy, or Divine Consciousness, that is the opposite of rationality. We also have to believe that it supports us, guides us, and actually *is* us. That takes a great deal of faith, as I experienced when I chose to go for pizza. We must dismiss the resistant reactions of the mind. But if we don't try using our intuition, we won't know its powerful existence as our source of guidance.

Some people seem to be born with a natural sense of intuition, but all of us can develop it. I have worked to hone my intuition—inviting, embracing, and acting on intuitive information—and I am also someone who just receives a lot of it. But because intuitive ability is in everyone, it can be developed by anyone. The wisdom of God is within us. The first step is to want this ability and be open to listening to it.

To live from intuition is also about surrendering our ego to faith. I have lived intuitively for so long that I can no longer act on something unless I have peace inside and "know that I know." I have come to trust my intuition more than I trust my own thoughts.

What are some reasons that we are hesitant to trust intuition?

First, it is illogical not to think about something and to just wait for some invisible force to provide answers. It goes against everything human.

Second, intuitive guidance means we didn't come up with the answer, so our egos can't feel good or take credit. Yet when we begin to trust something more than we trust our egos, it helps the ego fade. When the ego is not fed, it dies.

Third, too often we don't pay attention to the "bizarre" stuff. We've all had experiences of intuition, we just haven't all grabbed onto those experiences with the desire to know more. Sometimes we may even embrace our gut wisdom, but then we go back into the realm of the mind and dismiss it.

The first rule for honing intuition is to be willing to be in a neutral state. We need to have no preconceived ideas about answers or outcomes. Remember, intuition is a gift. Surprise! Intuition comes from living in expectancy without having expectations. We know the answer will come, but we have no preset idea or desire about what the answer will be. The art of intuition involves trust that God will guide us, sometimes without even a hint as to where we are going or what we are doing. When that happens, it is like having a blindfold on or buying ingredients before we know what we are baking. At other times, our intuition works by means of hints and nudges along the way.

In trusting, we may be led to something better than we had imagined, something different or even something we don't want at first. But trust means that we open ourselves to something beyond what we can see or discern. It's trust for the whole trip, not just the first leg of it.

How do we know it's the voice of God on the line and not just our own thoughts? One way to discern that is whether or not fear accompanies it. Our voices usually come with fear. They are whiny, judgmental, or tense, and they create even more stress. They are often demanding with an "ought to" tone, and they can feel confused or self-justifying.

Consider a time when you may have taken a leap of faith and suddenly began wondering what the heck you had just done. You worried that it wouldn't work, that you'd lose money, or that you'd make a fool of yourself. The mind bombards us with negative thoughts. But intuition comes calmly. It is peaceful, and it simply feels right. It is clear, certain, and spontaneous. Suddenly you just have a feeling that you know what is right. That's the voice and feeling you can trust, and the way to know it is to try it. It would be great if it were provable by science, but it isn't. That's actually the cool thing about intuition. It's just plain deep, and it doesn't come from us.

Also, when we are listening to the mind, it feels like it is physically in our heads. But when we are listening to our spirits, the sensation comes in our gut or through a sense of expansion in the chest. The mind is head-knowledge and the gut is spiritual wisdom.

The statement "I feel it in my gut" indicates a profound knowing inside. We can also hear a literal voice, as I did when I was told to take my kids out for pizza. The voice of God may come as a physical sensation or from someone else's words. You may be talking with a group and someone shares, "I decided to move first and then look for a job. I wanted to feel at home in my environment rather than have the job be the decider." And that was what you needed to hear. Intuition kicks in, you feel a *yes* when you hear the words, and the words become a message, seemingly just for you.

Even though I didn't pursue it until I was desperate, I have always known and sensed something other than life in the tangible realm. When I pursued it, deep intuitive connections began to happen. I frequently just know things, and I feel a profound sense of wisdom coming from my core. My intuition sometimes operates through images. A picture will come to my mind from out of nowhere. When it happens that way, it is usually an insight for someone else. Another way I receive intuition is from words that appear as if a banner were marching through my mind with a message.

Intuition makes itself known and felt in many ways. We may see pictures or hear words, as I sometimes do. We may feel a flow of warmth through our bodies, a thought may appear like a neon sign, or we may experience goose bumps. Intuition means that we just know something but we don't know why. On the opposite side of the spectrum, a feeling of heaviness or anxiety, a tight jaw or nervousness, are also aspects of intuition. These signs show us not to do something.

After an airplane crash, we sometimes hear stories of people who say they had a strong feeling not to get on that plane and heeded their intuition. Why did they get that intuition and someone else didn't? There are unseen and unknown plans for everything and everyone in life.

At times the knowing comes when we are reading and certain words seem to jump off the page. Or we may dream an answer to a problem we are currently having. The best way to decipher how intuition works for you individually is to remember how it happened when you just knew or even thought that God was telling you something. If you've never felt that God was giving you information or guidance, just be aware of when you have a sense of rightness or certainty about something but it doesn't feel like your normal sense of knowing. You may even wonder where that thought or idea came from.

One way to develop intuition is to write down all the problems we need answered in a notebook or journal. Then ask for guidance and let it go.

I have done this for over twenty years and now have the joy and comfort of seeing God's answers and timing. At one point in my life, I wanted to know where to move. I was living in Atlanta and felt it was time to leave, so I entered the question and date of it: March 22, 2000. On July 7, as I was flying back to Atlanta from Chicago after a family vacation, I was looking out the plane window at the clouds, and I heard, *Go home and start packing.* I asked where I was going, but the same words were repeated in my mind: *Go home and start packing.* I wanted an answer, but I didn't get it, so I just followed the command.

I began in the dining room of my apartment and was halfway through packing the living room when a second thought came. *Go to St. Louis and check it out.*

My sister and her family lived there and my parents lived with them, so I drove out. I found a great two-bedroom apartment down the street from their home. Of course, there were underlying reasons for the move. Being by family again would help me uncover buried memories of a lot of family abuse. With sad clarity, I began to see where I stood in my family and how much I had allowed to go unchecked. Their behavior hit me in the face, and it was a perfect example of having to repeat a lesson when it wasn't learned the first time. It was just the beginning of a long road of remembering, and it was both painful and powerful. The timing and place of my move were perfect.

We can put our needs out there and wait, knowing that we've been heard. And there is no need to worry that you may not hear the answer because intuitive guidance rarely speaks just one time. If we don't hear it, it will speak again. Everything always eventually gets answered in the right way and at the right time. By writing it down and putting a date alongside the problem or request, we can begin to understand and relax into the fact that God has a timeline, and it always works out fine.

Our first steps are baby steps. You may feel pulled to go to a certain store without knowing why. Then something happens there, and you come to see the reason for your intuitive guidance. Or perhaps you feel an urge to do something that doesn't even make sense. Do it. But there is one thing to know about intuitive guidance. It never goes for the negative. It never guides us to misbehave or do the wrong thing.

The practice of developing intuition might go like this: You get an idea. It comes from nowhere. It feels a bit like it might be from God, or maybe it simply doesn't feel like you. That's another sure sign that you must listen. Try not to figure out what it means. Just do what the thought says to do. If you don't practice, you won't learn. Ask to start with the little things.

In the beginning, you may get it wrong. But it's like practicing the piano. You learn the keys and the sounds. You learn the tempo. Pretty soon you are totally aware of how to move your hands and what the notes sound like. That's how we learn the voice of God. Reassurance comes even if we are going in the wrong direction because when we have made a sincere commitment to listen to Spirit, we will be redirected.

Often, we receive an intuitive answer, but our minds argue with it. I was sharing a concern I had about a relative with my son and he said, "I think having to do this won't be bad but will actually help him." Then he immediately said, "Or maybe it won't be good." His intuition had given him the answer as soon as I shared what was happening, and then his mind barged in to take the answer away.

When you get your spontaneous input, don't listen to the mind or let it take the answer away. Follow that instant first thought. Argue if you must, but follow the intuition anyway. After all, the mind cannot see down the road or into tomorrow. We, the mind or ego, do not have a bird's-eye view. The mind doesn't know all the players in a scenario, and certainly the mind isn't all-knowing. God is. Living in synchronicity with Spirit can be scary, but it is always rewarding.

When I quit a writing job because I was hitting a glass ceiling, I said aloud in faith, "It is so wrong to be treated like this. I have to leave. God has a plan. I trust that there is a plan." My heart and my gut knew I was doing the right thing though my head insisted that I had no other job to go to and was being really stupid. But isn't that the bigger faith? Doing something when you don't know the outcome or have a backup plan? So I told my boss I was going to leave.

As I was walking through the lobby, headed back to my office after giving my boss the news, a man accidently bumped into me and apologized. But then he followed me to my office and said, "Excuse me. I'm looking for someone to help me write my company's publications. Can you tell me where I might find someone?"

Yep. God had a plan before I even had a chance to worry about it.

A woman once asked me how I know that intuition is guiding me rather than my mind. My answer was that I have practiced knowing the sound and feel of Spirit. I've learned the difference between the voice of Mary's mind and the voice of God. I've also developed the courage to avoid trying to figure things out, to just take action and wait for an answer. Nothing in the universe has to be solved immediately. The urgency of *now* is the mind. When in doubt, don't do anything. As one Zen poem says, "Sitting quietly, doing nothing, spring comes, and grass grows by itself."

We have the opportunity to live as human beings having isolated spiritual experiences of or with God. Or we have the opportunity to be who we really are: spiritual beings having an earthly experience. Spiritual beings have the ability to walk life's journey without thoughts about themselves or about problems. When we choose to live by intuition every minute of every day, we are on that road.

To have no thought of themselves means to have no attachment to the things that happen or don't happen. This is vital. The goal is to live in observation mode so our minds do not do the dictating. Then we begin to marvel at all the little things that come together: a phone call to cheer us up, the perfect pair of jeans on sale, the arrival of a book we've been wanting to read. Little things bring joy. And the big things come too: the perfect job, a new car, the love of your life. Each day is filled with surprises and gifts if we are aware that it is God in us and as us inspiring the things that happen. When we quit trying to make things happen, life begins to flow.

Recently, I submitted some writing to a publisher and had not heard back, even after leaving messages. Some remnants of my ego-self really wanted the publisher to purchase my work, and it wasn't happening. The mind is always hanging around trying to snag us, but we get faster and faster at not taking the bait. Picture a fishing pole with a piece of lush, rich chocolate on the end. It's being swung back and forth in front of us. It makes you want to grab it, doesn't it? This tempting picture is just a thought. Don't.

Remembering whose life it was, I sat down, surrendered, and said, "Okay. I'll let it go. If it's not meant for them to buy my writing, that's okay too." The next morning, I got a call asking for five of my stories. The formula: I got out of the way, surrendered to any outcome, and flow just happened.

Intuition may feel risky when we first start using it, but it will become our best friend. This is because intuition is from Source, which knows everything: the future, the plan, the timing, the rightness, the best life fit. We do not need to live in our minds when we can expand to having life be a constant gift. We just need to be willing to trust our inner selves and act on our guidance. We must pull back from the mind's efforts to override our wisdom. To develop intuition, it is helpful to be in touch with our senses and become aware of the messages coming at us.

When we let intuition be our guide, we open our lives to the flow of a plan divinely created for us. And when we do that, our lives have peace and ease. Everything falls into place when we just let it happen in its own way and time.

Practice

List reasons to distrust intuition. List reasons to trust intuition. Which reasons to distrust and/or trust are the most persuasive? Which ones do you connect with most?

Remember a time when you had a gut feeling:
    What was it?
    How did it come to you?
    How did it feel?
    Did you follow it?
    What happened?

Which of these have you experienced?
    Hunches
    Gut feelings
    A knowing beyond reason
    Feeling like it's right
    Being in the flow
    Words from a person, book, or song that answered a question
    A sentence popping out from a book opened at random
    A thought that felt like a neon sign
    A thought that was gentle and quiet and came from nowhere
    Goose bumps
    Peaceful feelings in the heart area
    Magical coincidences or synchronicity

Images or pictures in the mind
Dreams
Sensations in the body (pit in the stomach, tingling, excitement, anxiety)
Heaviness or lightness
Directives: a thought that came strongly to or through you

Getting real:
What would you do if you didn't like Spirit's answer?
What would you do if there was a deadline but the answer wasn't there yet?

CHAPTER FOURTEEN

My Awakening

I AM NOT A GREAT RELIGIOUS LEADER. On my journey, my only qualifications have been my appetite for truth and the experiences that have shown me that truth. In my pursuit, I let my sense of self be shredded. Some of my hunger has arisen because life has been so painful, and some has arisen because my heart knows there is infinitely more than my mind can grasp. In the end, I wanted God more than I wanted myself.

On July 8, 2009, I got into bed to read and looked at the clock. It was 9:04 p.m. With my book in hand, I rested back on the pillows while looking forward to beginning a new Harlan Coben novel. One second I was just "me," leaning back and getting ready to read, and the next, I was suddenly and unexpectedly sitting straight up, but no longer "me." I did not know this shift would be coming. Yet it happened in a way that was as simple and natural as breathing. I simply and completely woke up from the illusion of a "self," and words came forth. "Oh! I am God. I have always been God. I will always be God. All the life I have spent suffering, all of the time I have spent seeking . . . and I have always been only an expression of God."

In an instant, I knew there is only One Life in many forms. One was God as Mary, experiencing a human life that I had once believed was mine. But it was God's life, and there *was* no "me." I had a sudden and deep understanding that I had no guilt, no regrets, and I, the self called Mary, had never suffered. I was suddenly shown my life as though I were looking over my left shoulder and panning back to infancy.

A voice within me said, *Look back at your life. It was me that both loved and endured all of it. It was me experiencing the life I planned and created as Mary.*

Nothing had ever been done by me or would ever be done by me. I had always been only the perfect life of God expressed as Mary. That was it. Unexpectedly, there was no longer a "me." A personal "I" never was and never would be. It was a spontaneous awakening from the illusion of a self in which I had always lived. From that instant on, a personal feeling of Mary was gone.

There was no sense of pride about the enlightenment because there was no sense of it being "me." When I tried to reach inside to feel my old sense of self, I could not find her.

As Gary Crowley shared in his book, *From Here to Here*:

> A King and a sage died at the same time and ended up facing God together.
>
> "When you said, 'I am God,' it angered me," God said to the King. "I cannot allow you the highest place in the afterlife."
>
> "When you said, 'I am God,' I felt loved," God said to the sage. "I'm granting you the highest place in the afterlife."

"Why are you treating us differently if we both said the same thing?" asked the King.

"When you said, 'I am God,' you were talking about you," sighed God. "When the sage said, 'I am God,' he was talking about me."

I had known for many years about Oneness and had known that I was the expression of God, but it had been in my head and perhaps even in my heart. I had not known it as my entire existence. Through years of spiritual growth and experiences, I realized I was a spiritual being having a human experience, but the human had never quite disappeared. Now she was gone completely.

I put my feet on the floor, got out of bed, and said out loud, "Look at God's feet walking across the carpet!" At the bathroom mirror, I said, "Look at God looking at herself." All of a sudden, I was big and completely present as all that was. The "I" had no need to become anything because that "I" was already everything. And with that came the full-blown realization that I was not in control of anything. And control didn't matter. There was also a feeling of great compassion for myself, the one who had lived as the struggling Mary for so many years. As God, I unconditionally loved who I had always been.

The next morning, I sat on my deck looking at the mountains. Leaning against the wood siding of my condo, I crossed my legs and stared. I simply existed in the midst of all creation. There was no longer a Mary who felt separate from what she gazed upon. I just was. I was simply pure being.

All sense of control vanished, and when I tried to think, I couldn't. There was nothing to think about.

There was no one to pray to, nothing to ask for. All I could do was be, and in that being there was only curiosity about what would happen next.

During that time of no-self, I was shown that God loved being a simple rock in a river with cold water rolling over his back. He embraced the experience of being a father who had lost his son. God created all that is and all that happens to experience all that he can of himself.

The following night I attended a lecture by a Native American elder who was speaking about the Ute Indians. They had inhabited the Yampa Valley, where I lived in Steamboat Springs, Colorado. Since I had always felt a connection to Native Americans, I was interested to hear what he would say.

As a professional presentation coach and trainer, I was immediately aware that this gentleman had no formal training in speaking. The information was worth listening to, but his style was not polished. As I experienced my reactions to him, I simultaneously became aware of how much love I felt for him. He was the perfect expression of God sharing his life. There was no need to be eloquent. He was perfect as he was. I was awestruck by the love and acceptance I had for him as the perfect person to be voicing this message. I was also struck by the fact that I was not judging Mary for observing his lack of presentation skills. I was watching his presentation as God and not just as a human Mary.

This also made me cognizant of the fact that my human reactions and thoughts had not vanished. Even though I knew I was God as Mary, I (as God) had thoughts and feelings. God was truly having a human experience as me. It felt as though I were living on two levels at the same time. On the surface I had all of the normal "human" perspectives and emotions, but underneath, I felt the constant and deeper vibration of being, accompanied by unconditional love.

Everything was different, and yet nothing had changed. I looked, felt, and thought like Mary, and yet to the core of my being, there was no "me." Wants and desires existed, as did likes and dislikes, but underneath those elementary feelings, there flowed a calm knowing that my personal reactions could impact nothing and everything at the same time. I vibrated, echoing the words of the hymn, "All Is Well with My Soul."

The following week I attended my spiritual book club, where I normally contributed ideas to the discussion. But that evening, I had nothing to say. I was no longer seeking and no longer trying to find meaning, nor did I care about figuring anything out. For the major portion of the evening, I just observed the many ways my friends tried to approach what or who they already were—God. I had lived in that role of the seeker, and it felt odd to be so content.

Towards the end of the evening, a sudden desire to share my experience arose. I checked with my inner being and then sensed that if I was supposed to share my awakening with the group, someone would say the word *dualism*. Within minutes, three group members began an exchange of ideas using the word *dualism* five times.

I raised my hand to speak and began to share my extraordinary story.

This state of not-Mary didn't stay permanently. It lasted two weeks, and then I began to feel like the human Mary again. The awakening had not shut down, but the ability to be and live it in such a powerful and complete way had lessened. I had experienced a full awakening in which there was no self. When it faded, the full truth of the experience remained, and the process of becoming it again did not stop.

I continued to open to the truth of no-self more easily and to feel life from a nondual place. I became even looser with life and let things go more easily.

Then, ten years later, I sat straight up again. It was at a book club meeting. It had been over thirty years since I had first read the mystical teacher Joel Goldsmith, and I was led to a group studying him. We had been reading and sharing his books for months, and we were currently studying *Practicing the Presence*. We all knew what awakening was, yet the group was clinging to the learning phase of trying to wake up. They kept thinking and acting as though they still had a personal self to get rid of. I was feeling myself in a different place. I was engaging in the discussion while simultaneously observing the thoughts and experiences of others.

As this continued, a sudden and powerful realization came forth. Hashing out and talking about behaviors was feeding the sense of self, and it made me exhausted. I didn't want to try to unravel anything more about a separate Mary. I knew I was already awake. That sense of a Mary had been hashed out of me, and I was finished.

One evening after our group's opening meditation, I spontaneously sat straight up and said, "I can't do this anymore. I can't keep trying to be awake. I am awake. I am the expression of the Creator, and I'm tired of keeping this separate Mary alive by working on her. It's time to let this expression touch other lives. It's time to let God express as Mary. Just the act of struggling to get rid of her keeps her alive. I'm done with that."

My awakening had come full circle. Just as had happened in 2009, I was fully awake again, only now it was with full awareness of "myself as an expression" that I saw, felt, and experienced life.

As I live, there is no sense of owning what is happening. There is no "Mary" in me, no ego-attachment or personal sense of self. It is similar to what happens when we try to find the mind: We can't find it. It isn't anywhere. When I look, I can't find Mary anymore.

Living in Colorado, I have grown to love aspen trees. I can sit outdoors surrounded by aspens and just bathe in the beauty and calm. Yet an aspen, or any other tree, is not a tree because we name it one. The word is confining and limiting. A tree is a creation, an expression in form with a place in the universe that is specific to where it is physically. We can imagine all its purposes, enjoy its shade, and wonder at its leaves. But we really have no concept of the thing, outside of the words we use to give it meaning from a human perspective. What does God call it?

The world is God's imagination. We are not the limited humans we cling to as our selves. We aren't us because we are bestowed with a name, a gender, or a role. We are the perfect and imperfect expressions of Creation. Life expresses itself in us and as us. Life is meant to flow.

The choice to let go of our belief in separation allows for the fullness of Life to flow, using guidance and wisdom from within. Life goes far beyond the mind that has controlled and limited our perceptions. We are not the version of ourselves that we have all created.

The challenge is to listen to the voice of Spirit inside us more than we listen to our deceptive minds. The only path to freedom proceeds by way of surrender, death, and loss of self. It is also the path of peace. Truth comes to life when we let go and get out of the way. As long as we think we are separate from God, we will never see or be the truth. One truly has to die to be born again.

We can walk asleep or we can walk awake. We can be the creations that we are intended to be by seeking and learning to live from the inside out. In so doing, we die to the belief in a separate self.

Live in an illusion, or be the truth. The choice is yours. We have been so programmed to believe in our personal selves that it is a powerful challenge to let the programmed belief go. But you can step outside of the box of everything you thought was truth and ask God to direct your path, guide you to who you really are, and bless you with the freedom and peace that comes of surrender.

Life is meant to be experienced with and as love. It is ours to receive and embrace. You are more than you can ever imagine.

Acknowledgments

FIRST AND FOREMOST, I want to thank my illusion of self for her ability to keep seeking even through the worst times, for her hunger to find the truth, and for giving herself up when she did find the truth. I want to thank Shirley Allmon for carrying the burden of my journey when I couldn't, my children Ron Nelson, Carrie Mancuso, and Jennifer Calhoun for being amazing, strong and loving children, Joel Goldsmith for taking the journey and writing the books that helped me understand there is only God, David Gantt for his years of support and care in the toughest of times, and Terry Hickman for being the unconditional love I was always intended to know. I also want to thank Joya Stevenson for her insights on content, Melanie Mulhall for her ability to help me form my message, and Bob Schram for his intuitive creativity.

About the Author

MARY NELSON is a a spiritual intuitive, award-winning writer and speaker, as well as a spiritual and life coach. With unbridled enthusiasm for pushing the envelope of life's journey, she brings energy, commitment and passion to her work of helping individuals achieve their greatest joy, peace and fulfillment. Mary conducts life-transforming coaching sessions and workshops to help people begin or deepen their personal and spiritual journeys.

In her career as a consultant to Fortune 500 companies, she coached managers and executives on their presentation skills, communications and team building. As a writer, Mary has been a newspaper columnist, reporter, and feature writer. She has a degree in psychology and a master's in adult education.

Mary resides in Steamboat Springs, Colorado where she loves to play in nature skiing, biking, and hiking.

Find out more at: mary-nelson.com

www.ingramcontent.com/pod-product-compliance
Lightning Source LLC
Chambersburg PA
CBHW032041290426
44110CB00012B/897